# Kibana 7 Quick Start

Visualize your Elasticsearch data with ease

**Anurag Srivastava**

**BIRMINGHAM - MUMBAI**

# Kibana 7 Quick Start Guide

Copyright © 2019 Packt Publishing

**Commissioning Editor:** Amey Varangaonkar
**Acquisition Editor:** Aditi Gour
**Content Development Editor:** Mohammed Yusuf Imaratwale
**Technical Editor:** Ralph Rosario
**Copy Editor:** Safis Editing
**Project Coordinator:** Kinjal Bari
**Proofreader:** Safis Editing
**Indexer:** Mariammal Chettiyar
**Graphics:** Alishon Mendonsa
**Production Coordinator:** Aparna Bhagat

First published: January 2019

Production reference: 1310119

Published by Packt Publishing Ltd.
Livery Place
35 Livery Street
Birmingham
B3 2PB, UK.

ISBN 978-1-78980-403-4

www.packtpub.com

*To my mom; my dad; my wife, Chanchal; and my son, Anvit. Without the support of Chanchal, I wouldn't have been able to complete this book on time.*

*– Anurag Srivastava*

`mapt.io`

Mapt is an online digital library that gives you full access to over 5,000 books and videos, as well as industry leading tools to help you plan your personal development and advance your career. For more information, please visit our website.

# Why subscribe?

- Spend less time learning and more time coding with practical eBooks and Videos from over 4,000 industry professionals

- Improve your learning with Skill Plans built especially for you

- Get a free eBook or video every month

- Mapt is fully searchable

- Copy and paste, print, and bookmark content

# Packt.com

Did you know that Packt offers eBook versions of every book published, with PDF and ePub files available? You can upgrade to the eBook version at `www.packt.com` and as a print book customer, you are entitled to a discount on the eBook copy. Get in touch with us at `customercare@packtpub.com` for more details.

At `www.packt.com`, you can also read a collection of free technical articles, sign up for a range of free newsletters, and receive exclusive discounts and offers on Packt books and eBooks.

# Contributors

## About the author

**Anurag Srivastava** is a senior technical lead and has more than 12 years of experience. He is proficient in designing architecture for scalable and highly available applications. He has handled development teams and several clients from all around the globe in the last 10 years of his professional career. He is experienced with using the Elastic stack (Elasticsearch, Logstash, and Kibana) to create dashboards using system metrics data, log data, application data, and relational databases.

# About the reviewer

**Giacomo Veneri** (1973) was born in Siena, Italy. He is an expert on data processing and Industrial Internet of Things. Working actively as a digital manager, he is the author of several books, including *Maven Build Customization* and *Hands-on Industrial Internet of Things*. He graduated from the University of Siena in Computer Science in 1999, and received his PhD in 2014 in neuroscience and neural computation.

# Packt is searching for authors like you

If you're interested in becoming an author for Packt, please visit `authors.packtpub.com` and apply today. We have worked with thousands of developers and tech professionals, just like you, to help them share their insight with the global tech community. You can make a general application, apply for a specific hot topic that we are recruiting an author for, or submit your own idea.

# Table of Contents

# Preface

Kibana is an open source data exploration and visualization platform. It is part of Elastic Stack, where we have Elasticsearch, Logstash, and Beats, along with Kibana. Using Kibana, we can explore data visually and can analyze it in real time. Kibana enables us to implement APM for application performance monitoring and Timelion enables us to play with time-series data. Then we have Dev Tools, by means of which we can run Elasticsearch queries direct from the Kibana interface. We have ML, by means of which we can predict future trends or ascertain anomalies in the data. Kibana provides us with Reporting, through which we can export CSV or PDF reports, Monitoring, to get insights into the complete Elastic Stack, and Watcher, to alert you in the event of any issue with the data.

Kibana, along with other Elastic Stack components, provides us with full-stack monitoring capability. Using Beats, we can get system metrics, log data, packet data, and so on. Logstash enables us to retrieve data from any other possible sources, including DBMS, CSV, or any other third-party tool, and then, using APM, we can fetch application data to monitor application performance. In this way, using Kibana, we can have an end-to-end monitoring system where a single dashboard can show all key performance indicators.

This book is there to help you understand the core concepts and the practical implementations, by means of which you can start using Kibana for a variety of use cases. It covers how to ingest data from different sources, using Beats or Logstash, into Elasticsearch, and then how to explore, analyze, and visualize it in Kibana. It covers how to play with time-series data to create complex graphs using Timelion and show them on your dashboard along with other visualizations, and then how to embed your dashboard or visualization on a web page. You will also learn about APM to monitor your application by installing and configuring the APM server and APM agents. We have also covered different X-Pack features, such as user and role management under security, alerting, monitoring, and ML. This book will also explain how to create ML jobs to find anomalies in your data.

# Who this book is for

This book is for anybody who wants to explore data. We used to obtain data from different sources, which can be scattered. Using Kibana, we can arrange, analyze, and visualize it, and can then retrieve the relevant information from that diffuse data. For this book, no prior knowledge is required, and anyone can start working on Kibana using the simple introduction and practical implementations in the book. In this book, the focus is on a practical approach, where aspects are explained using practical examples, images, and a stepwise approach, where you need to sequentially follow a number of steps in order to achieve something. In this way, it is quite easy to understand the topics and you can easily implement the given steps

# What this book covers

Chapter 1, *Introducing Kibana*, introduces Elastic Stack, where we explain the different components of Elastic Stack, including Elasticsearch, Logstash, Kibana, and different Beats. The introduction is followed by an explanation of the different use cases of Elastic Stack, including System Performance Monitoring, where we monitor system performance, Log Management, where we collect different logs and monitor them from a central location, Application Performance Monitoring, where we monitor our application by connecting it to a central APM server, Application Data Analysis, where we analyze the application data, Security Monitoring and Alerting, where we can secure our stack using X-Pack and monitor it regularly, while also being able to configure alerts to keep an eye on any change that may impact system performance, and finally Data Visualization, where we use Kibana to create different types of visualizations using available data.

Chapter 2, *Getting Data into Kibana*, covers different ways to get data in Elasticsearch. We examine how Beats can be installed on a server to send data, since they are lightweight data shippers. Under Beats, we cover Filebeat, for reading file data, including apache logs, system logs, and application logs, and can then send these logs to Elasticsearch directly or using Logstash. We configure Metricbeat to read system metrics, such as CPU usage, memory usage, MySQL metrics, and Packetbeat, by means of which we can read network packet data to glean insights from it. After that, we cover how Logstash can be used to get the data and apply filters before sending it to Elasticsearch.

In the first section, we cover how to fetch CSV data using Logstash, where we pass a CSV file as input and specify the columns to send the data to Elasticsearch. After that, we explain how to configure the JDBC plugin to fetch MySQL data by running the SQL statement and applying the tracking column, by means of which the incremental data can be fetched in Logstash. After reading the MySQL data, it is pushed to Elasticsearch for analysis. Using Beats and Logstash, we can push data into Elasticsearch but, in order to analyze and visualize the data, we need this data in Kibana and, for that, we have to create index patterns in Kibana. Once the index pattern is created, we can see the data under the Discover option in Kibana, where we can apply a filter, run queries, and select fields to display.

Chapter 3, *Exploring Data*, describes Kibana Discover, and how we can explore data using Discover. In the beginning, we cover how to discover your data by means of different options provided in Kibana Discover, including how to limit the number of fields to display in order to focus on the dataset, which is more relevant than the other not so relevant fields. Then, we discover how to expand a document display to check all available fields, along with the option to view surrounding documents and single documents. From this screen, we can also apply the filter to any field. Then, we cover different ways to dissect our data, including filtering the data by applying the time-based filter, filtering the data based on different document fields, and applying queries to your dataset. We then explore how to save the searched data so that this search data, along with filter options, can be available to us whenever we want to use them again. After saving the search data, we can also export it from Kibana and save it into a file that can later be imported back into Kibana.

Chapter 4, *Visualizing Data*, explains how to visualize the data once it is available in Kibana after creating the index pattern. We begin with basic charts, where we cover a number of chart creations, including the area chart, heat map, and pie chart. We also explain how we can transform one type of chart into other by taking the examples of the area chart, line chart, and bar chart in the same way that we can change a pie chart into a donut, or vice versa. After that, we delve into data tables, by means of which we can generate tabular visualizations of data in which we can add additional metrics columns, along with actual data columns. We then cover metric-type visualizations, where we can display some metric values and tag clouds, which can be used to display word clouds with a link to filter out the data accordingly.

Chapter 5, *X-Pack with Machine Learning*, explains how X-Pack adds additional features to the existing Elastic Stack setup. We begin with an introduction to X-Pack, followed by the X-Pack installation process. We then delve into the different features of XPack, such as security, by means of which we can secure our Elastic Stack. As regards security, we cover user and role management by creating users, and roles, and then assign roles to the users. Following on from security, we cover monitoring, from the perspective of both an overview and a detailed view, where we can see the search and indexing rate. We then cover alerting, where we configure watch to send alert notifications by email. Following on from alerting, we cover reporting, by means of which we can generate CSV or PDF reports and download them. Finally, we cover ML, by means of which we create single- and multi-metric jobs and analyze the data by finding the anomaly and predicting future trends.

Chapter 6, *Monitoring Applications with APM*, covers Elastic APM and explains how we can monitor an application. We begin with APM components, which are APM Agents, APM Servers, Elasticsearch, and Kibana. After that, we delve into each of them in detail. APM Agents are open source libraries that can be configured in any of the supported language/libraries. Currently, we have support for Django and flask frameworks for Python, Java, Go, Node.js, Rails, Rack, RUM - JS, and Go. We can configure them to send application metrics and errors to the APM Server. We then cover the APM Server, which is again an open source software written in Go. The principal task of the APM Server is to receive data from different APM Agents and send it to Elasticsearch Cluster. Elasticsearch takes the APM data, which can be viewed, searched, or analyzed in Elasticsearch. Once data is pushed in Elasticsearch, we can display it in Kibana using a dedicated APM UI or through the Kibana Dashboard.

Chapter 7, Kibana Advanced Tools, describes Timelion and Dev Tools, which are quite useful tools in Kibana. We begin with an introduction to Timelion, and then different functions that are available in Timelion, such as the .es() function to set the Elasticsearch data source, and its different parameters, such as index, metric, split, offset, fit, and time field. We then cover other functions, such as .static(), to create static lines on the x-axis, the .points() function to convert the graph into a point display, the .color() function to change the color of the plot, the .derivetive() function to plot the difference in value over time, the .label() function to set the label for data series, the .range() function to limit the graph display between a particular min and max range, and finally the .holt() function to forecast the future trend or to ascertain the anomaly in the data. For a complete reference of functions, we can refer to the help section in Timelion. We then cover the use cases of Timelion. After Timelion, we describe Dev Tools, by means of which we can do multiple things. After the introduction to Dev Tools, we cover different Dev Tools options, including Console, by means of which we can execute Elasticsearch queries and can get the response on the same page. We then examine the Search Profiler, through which we can profile any Elasticsearch query by getting the details of the query components. Finally, we look at Grok Debugger, where we can create the Grok Pattern to parse sample data, thereby enabling the unstructured sample data to be converted into structured data. This structured data can then be used for data analysis or visualization and suchlike.

# To get the most out of this book

To get the most out of this book, no prior knowledge is required. Anyone who wants to analyze their data can use this book to learn how to do so.

# Download the example code files

You can download the example code files for this book from your account at
`www.packt.com`. If you purchased this book elsewhere, you can visit
`www.packt.com/support` and register to have the files emailed directly to you.

You can download the code files by following these steps:

1. Log in or register at `www.packt.com`.
2. Select the **SUPPORT** tab.
3. Click on **Code Downloads & Errata**.
4. Enter the name of the book in the **Search** box and follow the onscreen instructions.

Once the file is downloaded, please make sure that you unzip or extract the folder using the latest version of:

- WinRAR/7-Zip for Windows
- Zipeg/iZip/UnRarX for Mac
- 7-Zip/PeaZip for Linux

The code bundle for the book is also hosted on GitHub at `https://github.com/PacktPublishing/Kibana-7-Quick-Start-Guide`. In case there's an update to the code, it will be updated on the existing GitHub repository.

We also have other code bundles from our rich catalog of books and videos available at `https://github.com/PacktPublishing/`. Check them out!

# Conventions used

There are a number of text conventions used throughout this book.

`CodeInText`: Indicates code words in text, database table names, folder names, filenames, file extensions, pathnames, dummy URLs, user input, and Twitter handles. Here is an example: "We can add the cloud ID of Elasticsearch under the Elastic Cloud section in the `metricbeat.yml` file."

A block of code is set as follows:

```
input
{
    file
    {
        path => "/var/log/apache.log"
        type => "apache-access"
        start_position => "beginning"
    }
}
filter
{
    grok
    {
        match => [ "message", "%{COMBINEDAPACHELOG}" ]
    }
}
output
{
    elasticsearch
    {
        hosts => ["localhost:9200"]
    }
}
```

Any command-line input or output is written as follows:

```
/usr/share/logstash/bin/logstash -f
/etc/logstash/conf.d/crimes.conf
```

**Bold**: Indicates a new term, an important word, or words that you see on screen. For example, words in menus or dialog boxes appear in the text like this. Here is an example: Select **System info** from the **Administration** panel.

Warnings or important notes appear like this.

Tips and tricks appear like this.

# Get in touch

Feedback from our readers is always welcome.

**General feedback**: If you have questions about any aspect of this book, mention the book title in the subject of your message and email us at customercare@packtpub.com.

**Errata**: Although we have taken every care to ensure the accuracy of our content, mistakes do happen. If you have found a mistake in this book, we would be grateful if you would report this to us. Please visit www.packt.com/submit-errata, selecting your book, clicking on the Errata Submission Form link, and entering the details.

**Piracy**: If you come across any illegal copies of our works in any form on the internet, we would be grateful if you would provide us with the location address or website name. Please contact us at copyright@packt.com with a link to the material.

**If you are interested in becoming an author**: If there is a topic that you have expertise in, and you are interested in either writing or contributing to a book, please visit authors.packtpub.com.

# Reviews

Please leave a review. Once you have read and used this book, why not leave a review on the site that you purchased it from? Potential readers can then see and use your unbiased opinion to make purchase decisions, we at Packt can understand what you think about our products, and our authors can see your feedback on their book. Thank you!

For more information about Packt, please visit packt.com.

# Introducing Kibana 1

Kibana is a dashboard tool that's easy to use and works closely with Elasticsearch. We can use Kibana for different use cases, such as system monitoring and application monitoring. Kibana isn't just a visualization tool, it also creates a complete monitoring ecosystem when we leverage the power of Elastic Stack. Here's a small example: you're working on a project where you can't tolerate any outrage, be it due to the database, application, system-related issues, or anything related to the application's performance. In a traditional monitoring system, you can monitor system performance, application logs, and so on. But with Kibana and Elastic Stack, we can do following:

- Configure Beats to monitor system metrics, database metrics, and log metrics
- Configure APM to monitor your application metrics and issues if your application platform is supported
- Configure the JDBC plugin of Logstash to pull RDBMS data into Elasticsearch to make it available to Kibana for creating visualizations on KPIs
- There are different third-party plugins that help us to get data from those sources, for example, you can use the Twitter plugin to get Twitter feeds
- You can create alerts for certain thresholds, so that whenever that situation occurs, you get alerts so you don't have to continuously monitor the application
- You can apply machine learning on your data to get data anomalies or future trends by analyzing the current dataset

# Elastic Stack

Kibana with Elastic Stack can be used to fetch data from different sources and filter, process, and analyze it to create meaningful dashboards. Elastic Stack has the following components:

- **Elasticsearch**: We can store data in Elasticsearch.
- **Logstash**: A data pipeline that we can use to read data from various sources, and can write it to various sources. It also provides a feature to filter the input data before sending it to output.
- **Kibana:** A graphical user interface that we can use to do a lot of things, which I will cover in this chapter.
- **Beats**: Lightweight data shippers that sit on different servers and send data to Elasticsearch directly or via Logstash:
    - Filebeat
    - Metricbeat
    - Packetbeat
    - Auditbeat
    - Winlogbeat
    - Heartbeat

The following diagram shows how Elastic Stack works:

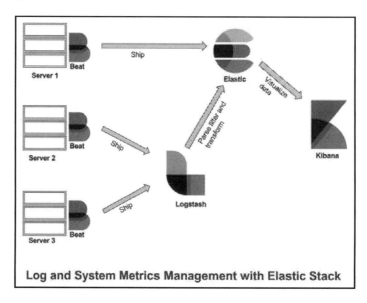

**Log and System Metrics Management with Elastic Stack**

In the preceding diagram, we have three different servers on which we have installed and configured Beats. These Beats are shipping data to Elasticsearch directly or via Logstash. Once this data is pushed into Elasticsearch, we can analyze, visualize, and monitor the data in Kibana. Let's discuss these components in detail; we're going to start with Elasticsearch.

# Elasticsearch

Elasticsearch is a full-text search engine that's primarily used for searching. It can also be used as a NoSQL database and analytics engine. Elasticsearch is basically schema-less and works in near-real-time. It has a RESTful interface, which helps us to interact with it easily from multiple interfaces. Elasticsearch supports different ways of importing various types of structured or unstructured data; it handles all types of data because of its schema-less behavior, and it's quite easy to scale. We have different clients available in Elasticsearch for the following languages:

- Java
- PHP
- Perl
- Python
- .NET
- Ruby
- JavaScript
- Groovy

Its query API is quite robust and we can execute different types of queries, such as boosting some fields over other fields, writing fuzzy queries, or searching on single or multiple fields, along with field search. Applying a Boolean search or wildcard search aggregation is another important feature of Elasticsearch, which helps us to aggregate different types of data; it has multiple types of aggregations, such as metric aggregation, bucket aggregation, and term aggregation.

 In fuzzy queries, we match words even then if there's no exact match for the spelling. For example, if we try to search a word with the wrong spelling, we can get the correct result using fuzzy search.

The architecture of Elasticsearch has the following components:

- **Cluster**: A collection of one or more nodes that work together is known as a cluster. By default, the cluster name is **elasticsearch**, which we can change to any unique name.
- **Node**: A node represents a single Elasticsearch server, which is identified by a universally unique identifier (**UUID**).
- **Index**: A collection of documents where each document in the collection has a common attribute.
- **Type**: A logical partition of the index to store more than one type of document. Type was supported in previous versions and is deprecated from 6.0.0 onward.
- **Document**: A single record in Elasticsearch is known as a document.
- **Shard**: We can subdivide the Elasticsearch index into multiple pieces, which are called shards. During indexing, we can provide the number of shards required.

Elasticsearch is primarily used to store and search data in the Elastic Stack; Kibana picks this data from Elasticsearch and uses it to analyzes or visualizes it in the form of charts and more, which can be combined to create dashboards.

# Logstash

Logstash is a data pipeline that can take data input from various sources, filter it, and output it to various sources; these sources can be files, Kafka, or databases. Logstash is a very important tool in Elastic Stack as it's primarily used to pull data from various sources and push it to Elasticsearch; from there, Kibana can use that data for analysis or visualization. We can take any type of data using Logstash, such as structured or unstructured data , which comes from various sources, such as the internet. The data can be transformed using Logstash's filter option, which has different plugins to play with different sets of data. For example, if we get an IP address in our data, the GeoIP plugin can add geolocation using that IP address, and in the output, we can get additional information of geolocation, which can then be used in Kibana to plot a map.

The following expression shows us an example of a Logstash configuration file:

```
input
{
    file
    {
        path => "/var/log/apache2/access.log"
    }
}
filter
```

```
{
    grok
    {
        match => {message => "%{COMBINEDAPACHELOG}"}
    }
}
output
{
    elasticsearch
    {
        hosts => "localhost"
    }
}
```

In the preceding expression, we have three sections: input, filter, and output. In the input section, we're reading the Apache access log file data. The filter section is there to extract Apache access log data in different fields, using the `grok` filter option. The output section is quite straightforward as it's pushing the data to the local Elasticsearch cluster. We can configure the input and output sections to read or write from or to different sources, whereas we can apply different plugins to transform the input data; for example, we can mutate a field, transform a field value, or add geolocation from an IP address using the filter option.

 Grok is a tool that we can use to generate structured and queryable data by parsing unstructured data.

# Kibana

In Elastic Stack, Kibana is mainly used to provide the graphical user interface, which we use to do multiple things. When Kibana was first released, we just used it to create charts and histograms, but with each update, Kibana evolves and now we have lots of killer features that make Kibana stand out from the crowd. There are many features in Kibana, but when we talk about the key features, they are as follows:

- Discover your data by exploring it
- Analyze your data by applying different metrics
- Visualize your data by creating different types of charts
- Apply machine learning on your data to get data anomaly and future trends

- Monitor your application using APM
- Manage users and roles
- A console to run Elasticsearch expressions
- Play with time-series data using Timelion
- Monitor your Elastic Stack using Monitoring

 **Application Performance Monitoring (APM)** is built on top of an Elastic Stack that we use to monitor application and software services in real time. We'll look at APM in more detail in `Chapter 6`, *Monitoring Applications with APM*.

In this way, there are different use cases that can be handled well using Kibana. I'm going to explain each of them in later chapters.

# Beats

Beats are single-purpose, lightweight data shippers that we use to get data from different servers. Beats can be installed on the servers as a lightweight agent to send system metrics, or process or file data to Logstash or Elasticsearch. They gather data from the machine on which they are installed and then send that data to Logstash, which we use to parse or transform the data before sending it to Elasticsearch, or we can send the Beats data directly into Elasticsearch.

They are quite handy as it takes almost no time to install and configure Beats to start sending data from the server on which they're installed. They're written to target specific requirements and work really well to solve use cases. Filebeat is there to work with different files like Apache log files or any other files, they keep a watch on the files, and as soon as an update happens, the updated data is shipped to Logstash or Elasticsearch. This file operation can also be configured using Logstash, but that may require some tuning; Filebeat is very easy to configure in comparison to Logstash.

Another advantage is that they have a smaller footprint and they sit on the servers from where we want the monitoring data to be sent. This makes the system quite simple because the collection of data happens on the remote machine, and then this data is sent to a centralized Elasticsearch cluster directly, or via Logstash. One more feature that makes Beats an important component of the Elastic Stack is the built-in Dashboard, which can be created in no time. We have a simple configuration in Beats to create a monitoring Dashboard in Kibana, which can be used to monitor directly or we might have to do some minor changes to use it for monitoring. There are different types of Beats, which we'll discuss here.

# Filebeat

Filebeat is a lightweight data shipper that forwards log data from different servers to a central place, where we can analyze that log data. Filebeat monitors the log files that we specify, collects the data from there in an incremental way, and then forwards them to Logstash, or directly into Elasticsearch for indexing.

After configuring Filebeat, it starts the input as per the given instructions. Filebeat starts a harvester to read a single log to get the incremental data for each separate file. Harvester sends the log data to libbeat, and then libbeat aggregates all events and sends the data to the output as per the given instructions like in Elasticsearch, Kafka, or Logstash.

# Metricbeat

Another lightweight data shipper that can be installed on any server to fetch system metrics. Metricbeat helps us to collect metrics from systems and services and to monitor the servers. Metrics are running on those servers, on which we installed Metricbeat. Metricbeat ships the collected system metrics data to Elasticsearch Logstash for analysis. Metricbeat can monitor many different services, as follows:

- MySQL
- PostgreSQL
- Apache
- Nginx
- Redis
- HAProxy

I've listed only some of the services, Metricbeat supports a lot more than that.

# Packetbeat

Packetbeat is used to analyze network packets in real time. Packetbeat data can be pushed to Elasticsearch, which we can use to configure Kibana for real-time application monitoring. Packetbeat is very effective in diagnosing network-related issues, since it captures the network traffic between our application servers and it decodes the application-layer protocols, such as HTTP, Redis, and MySQL. Also, it correlates the request and response, and captures important fields.

Packetbeat supports the following protocols:

- HTTP
- MySQL
- PostgreSQL
- Redis
- MongoDB
- Memcache
- TLS
- DNS

Using Packetbeat, we can send our network packet data directly into Elasticsearch or through Logstash. Packetbeat is a handy tool since it's difficult to monitor the network packet. Just install and configure it on the server where you want to monitor the network packets and start getting the packet data into Elasticsearch using which, we can create packet data monitoring dashboard. Packetbeat also provides a custom dashboard that we can easily configure using the Packetbeat configuration file.

# Auditbeat

Auditbeat can be installed and configured on any server to audit the activities of users and processes. It's a lightweight data shipper that sends the data directly to Elasticsearch or using Logstash. Sometimes it's difficult to track changes in binaries or configuration files; Auditbeat is helpful here because it detects changes to critical files, such as different configuration files and binaries.

We can configure Auditbeat to fetch audit events from the Linux audit framework. The Linux audit framework is an auditing system that collects the information of different events on the system. Auditbeat can help us to take that data and push it to Elasticsearch from where Kibana can be utilized to create dashboards.

# Winlogbeat

Winlogbeat is a data shipper that ships the Windows event logs to Logstash or the Elasticsearch cluster. It keeps a watch and reads from different Windows event logs and sends them to Logstash or Elasticsearch in a timely manner. Winlogbeat can send different types of events:

- Hardware Events
- Security Events

- System Events
- Application Events

Winlogbeat sends structured data to Logstash or Elasticsearch after reading raw event data to make it easy for filtering and aggregating the data.

## Heartbeat

Heartbeat is a lightweight shipper that monitors server uptime. It can be installed on a remote server; after that, it periodically checks the status of different services and tell us whether they're available. The major difference between Metricbeat and Heartbeat is that Metricbeat tells us whether that server is up or down, while Heartbeat tells us whether services are reachable—it's quite similar to the ping command, which tells us whether the server is responding.

# Use cases of Elastic Stack

There are many areas where we can use the Elastic Stack, such as logging where we mainly use Elastic Stack or for searching using Elasticsearch or for dashboarding for monitoring but these are just a few use case of the Elastic Stack which we primarily use, there are many other areas where we can use the power of Elastic Stack. We can use Elastic Stack for the following use cases:

- System Performance Monitoring
- Log Management
- Application Performance Monitoring
- Application Data Analysis
- Security Monitoring and Alerting
- Data Visualization

Let's discuss each of these in detail.

# System Performance Monitoring

When we run any application in production, we need to make it stable by avoiding anything that can impact the application's performance; this can be anything, such as the system, database, or any third-party dependencies, since if anything fails it impacts the application. In this section, we'll see how system monitoring can help us to avoid situations where the system can cause the application to outage.

Let's discuss the factors that can hamper application's performance. There can be number of reasons, such as the system memory or CPU creating a bottleneck because of an increase in user hits. In this situation, we can do multiple things, such as optimizing the application if it's possible and increasing the memory or CPU. We can do it to mitigate the outrage of the application, but it's only possible if we're monitoring the system metrics of the servers on which the application has been deployed. Using the monitoring, we can configure the alert whenever the threshold value of any component increases. In this way, you can protect yourself from any application outage because of system performance.

# Log Management

Log Management is one of the key use cases of Elastic Stack, and it has been primarily used for this purpose for many years. There are many benefits of log management using Elastic Stack, and I'll explain Elastic Stack simplifies things when it comes to monitoring logs. Let's say you have a log file and you need to explore it to get the root cause of the application outage – how are you going to proceed? Where will you open the file and what are you going to search and filter? We just need to push the log data into Elasticsearch and configure Kibana to read this data. We can use Filebeat to read the log files, such as Apache access and error logs. Apart from system logs, we can also configure Filebeat to capture application logs. Instead of Filebeat, we can use Logstash to take file data as input and output it to Elasticsearch.

# Application Performance Monitoring

Elastic Stack APM monitors applications and helps developers and system administrators monitor software applications for performance and availability. It also helps them to identify any current issues, or ones that may occur in the near future. Using APM, we can find and fix any bug in the code, as it makes the problems in the code searchable. By integrating APM with our code, we can monitor our code and make it better and more efficient. Elastic APM provides us with custom preconfigured dashboards in Kibana. We can integrate application data using APM and server stats, network details, and log details using Beats. This makes it easy to monitor everything in a single place.

We can apply machine learning to APM data by using the APM UI to find any abnormal behavior in the data. Alerts can also be applied to get an email notification if anything goes wrong in the code. Currently, Elastic APM supports Node.js, Python, Java, Ruby, Go, and JavaScript. It's easy to configure APM with your application and it requires only a few lines of code.

# Security, Monitoring, and Alerting with Elastic Stack

With X-Pack, we can enable security, alerting, and monitoring with our Elastic setup. These features are very important and we need them to protect our Elastic Stack from external access and any possible issues. Now let's discuss each of them in detail.

## Security

Security is a very important feature of X-Pack; without it, anyone can open the URL and access everything in Kibana, including index patterns, data, visualizations, and dashboards. During X-Pack installation and setup, we create the default user credentials. For security, we have role management and user management, using which we can restrict user access and secure the Elastic Stack.

## Monitoring

Monitoring provides us the insight on Elasticsearch, Logstash, and Kibana. Monitoring comes with X-Pack, which we can install after installing the basic Elastic Stack setup. Monitoring-related data is stored in Elasticsearch, which we can see from Kibana. We have built-in status warning in Kibana, custom alerts can be configured on data in the indices used for monitoring.

## Alerting

Elastic Stack uses alerting to keep an eye on any activity, such as whether CPU usage increases, memory consumption goes beyond some threshold, the response time of an application goes up, or 503 errors are increasing. By creating alerts, we can proactively monitor the system or application behavior and can apply a check before anything actually goes wrong.

Using alerts, we can notify every stakeholder without missing anything. We can apply alerts to detect specific issues, such as a user logged in from a different location, credit card numbers are showing in application logs, or the indexing rate of Elasticsearch increases. These are just some examples; we can apply alerts in so many cases.

There are different ways to notify the users, as there are lots of built-in integrations available for emails, slack, and so on. Apart from these built-in options, we can integrate alerts with any existing system by integrating the webhook output provided by Elastic Stack. Alerts also have simple template support, which we can use to customize the notification. I'll cover how we can configure the alerts in the coming chapters.

# Data Visualization

Data visualization is the main feature of Kibana and it's the best way to get information from the raw data. As we know, a picture tells a thousand words, so we can easily learn about a data trend by just seeing a simple chart. Kibana is popular because it has the ability to create dashboards for KPIs using data from different sources; we can even use Beats to get ready—made dashboards. We have different types of visualizations in Kibana, such as basic charts, data, time-series, and maps, which we'll cover in coming chapters. If we have data in Elasticsearch, we can create visualizations by creating index patterns in Kibana for those indexes in Elasticsearch.

# Installing Elastic Stack

Elastic Stack consists of different components, such as Elasticsearch, Logstash, Kibana, and different Beats. We need to install each component individually, so let's start with Elasticsearch.

 The installation steps might change, depending on the release of version 7. The updated steps will be available at the following link once the version is released.
https://www.packtpub.com/sites/default/files/downloads/InstallationofElasticStack7.pdf

# Elasticsearch

To install Elasticsearch 6, we need at least Java 8. Please ensure first that Java is installed with at least version 8 in your system. Once Java is installed, we can go ahead and install Elasticsearch. You can find the binaries at `www.elastic.co/downloads`.

## Installation using the tar file

Follow the steps to install using the tar file:

1. First, we need to download the latest Elasticsearch tar, as shown in the following code block:

```
curl -L -O
https://artifacts.elastic.co/downloads/elasticsearch/elasticsearch-
6.x.tar.gz
```

2. Then, extract it using the following command:

```
tar -xvf elasticsearch-6.x.tar.gz
```

3. After extracting it, we have a bunch of files and folders. Move to the `bin` directory by executing the following command:

```
cd elasticsearch-6.x/bin
```

4. After moving to the `bin` directory, run Elasticsearch using the following command:

```
./elasticsearch
```

## Installation using Homebrew

Using Homebrew, we can install Elasticsearch on macOS, as follows:

```
brew install elasticsearch
```

## Installation using MSI Windows installer

For Windows, we have the MSI Installer package, which includes a **graphical user interface (GUI)** that we can use to complete the installation process. We can download the Elasticsearch 6.x MSI from the Elasticsearch download section at `https://www.elastic.co/downloads/elasticsearch`.

We can launch the GUI-based installer by double-clicking on the downloaded executable file. On the first screen, select the deployment directories and install the software by following the installation screens.

# Installation using the Debian package

Follow the steps to install using the Debian package:

1. First, install the apt-transport-https package using the following command:

```
sudo apt-get install apt-transport-https
```

2. Save the repository definition on /etc/apt/sources.list.d/elastic-6.x.list:

```
echo "deb https://artifacts.elastic.co/packages/6.x/apt stable main" | sudo tee -a /etc/apt/sources.list.d/elastic-6.x.list
```

3. To install the Elasticsearch Debian package, run the following command:

```
sudo apt-get update && sudo apt-get install elasticsearch
```

# Installation with the RPM package

1. Download and then install the public signing key:

```
rpm --import https://artifacts.elastic.co/GPG-KEY-elasticsearch
```

2. Create a file called elasticsearch.repo for RedHat-based distributions under the /etc/yum.repos.d/ directory. For the OpenSuSE-based distributions, we have to create the file under the /etc/zypp/repos.d/ directory. We need to add the following entry in the file:

```
[elasticsearch-6.x]
name=Elasticsearch repository for 6.x packages
baseurl=https://artifacts.elastic.co/packages/6.x/yum
gpgcheck=1
gpgkey=https://artifacts.elastic.co/GPG-KEY-elasticsearch
enabled=1
autorefresh=1
type=rpm-md
```

After adding the preceding code, we can install Elasticsearch on the following environments.

- We can run the yum command on CentOS and older versions of RedHat-based distributions:

```
sudo yum install elasticsearch
```

- On Fedora and other newer versions of RedHat distributions, use the dnf command:

```
sudo dnf install elasticsearch
```

- The zypper command can be used on OpenSUSE-based distributions:

```
sudo zypper install elasticsearch
```

- The Elasticsearch service can be started or stopped using the following command:

```
sudo -i service elasticsearch start
sudo -i service elasticsearch stop
```

# Logstash

We have different ways to install Logstash based on the operating system. Let's see how we can install Logstash on different environments.

## Using APT Package Repositories

Follow the steps to install using APT Package Repositories

1. Install the Public Signing key, but before that download the APT package repository. You can do that using the following command:

```
wget -qO - https://artifacts.elastic.co/GPG-KEY-elasticsearch |
sudo apt-key add -
```

2. On Debian, we have to install the apt-transport-https package:

```
sudo apt-get install apt-transport-https
```

3. Save the following repository definition, under the `/etc/apt/sources.list.d/elastic-6.x.list` directory:

```
echo "deb https://artifacts.elastic.co/packages/6.x/apt stable
main" | sudo tee -a /etc/apt/sources.list.d/elastic-6.x.list
```

4. Run the `sudo apt-get update` command to update the repository. After the update, the repository will be ready to use. We can install Logstash by executing the following command:

```
sudo apt-get update && sudo apt-get install logstash
```

## Using YUM Package Repositories

Follow the steps to install using YUM Package Repositories:

1. Download the public signing key and then install it using the following expression:

```
rpm --import https://artifacts.elastic.co/GPG-KEY-elasticsearch
```

2. Under the `/etc/yum.repos.d/` directory, add the following expression in a file with a `.repo` suffix, for example. See the following code block in the `logstash.repo` file:

```
[logstash-6.x]
name=Elastic repository for 6.x packages
baseurl=https://artifacts.elastic.co/packages/6.x/yum
gpgcheck=1
gpgkey=https://artifacts.elastic.co/GPG-KEY-elasticsearch
enabled=1
autorefresh=1
type=rpm-md
```

3. The repository is ready after we add the preceding code. Using the following command, we can install Logstash:

```
sudo yum install logstash
```

# Kibana

From version 6.0.0 onward, Kibana only supports 64-bit operating systems, so we need to ensure we have a 64-bit operating system before installing Kibana.

# Installing Kibana with .tar.gz

Follow the steps to install Kibana with `.tar.gz`

1. Using the following expression, we can download and install the Linux archive for Kibana v6.x:

```
wget
https://artifacts.elastic.co/downloads/kibana/kibana-6.x-linux-x86_
64.tar.gz
tar -xzf kibana-6.1.3-linux-x86_64.tar.gz
```

2. Change the directory and move to `$KIBANA_HOME` by running the following command:

```
cd kibana-6.1.3-linux-x86_64/
```

3. We can start Kibana using the following command:

```
./bin/kibana
```

# Installing Kibana using the Debian package

Follow the steps to install Kibana using the Debian package:

1. For the Debian package, download and install the public signing key using the following command:

```
wget -qO - https://artifacts.elastic.co/GPG-KEY-elasticsearch |
sudo apt-key add -
```

2. Install the `apt-transport-https` package using the following expression:

```
sudo apt-get install apt-transport-https
```

3. We need to add the following repository definition under `/etc/apt/sources.list.d/elastic-6.x.list`:

```
echo "deb https://artifacts.elastic.co/packages/6.x/apt stable
main" | sudo tee -a /etc/apt/sources.list.d/elastic-6.x.list
```

4. Install the Kibana Debian package, by running the following command:

```
sudo apt-get update && sudo apt-get install kibana
```

# Installing Kibana using RPM

Follow the steps to install Kibana using RPM:

1. Install the public signing key after downloading it for the RPM package:

   ```
   rpm --import https://artifacts.elastic.co/GPG-KEY-elasticsearch
   ```

2. Create a file called `kibana.repo` under the `/etc/yum.repos.d/` directory for RedHat-based distributions. For OpenSuSE-based distributions, we need to create the file under the `/etc/zypp/repos.d/` directory and then add the following expression:

   ```
   [kibana-6.x]
   name=Kibana repository for 6.x packages
   baseurl=https://artifacts.elastic.co/packages/6.x/yum
   gpgcheck=1
   gpgkey=https://artifacts.elastic.co/GPG-KEY-elasticsearch
   enabled=1
   autorefresh=1
   type=rpm-md
   ```

After adding the preceding expression in our file, we can install Kibana using the following commands:

- On `yum`, CentOS, and older RedHat-based distributions, we need to run the following command:

  ```
  sudo yum install kibana
  ```

- We can use the `dnf` command on Fedora and newer RedHat distributions:

  ```
  sudo dnf install kibana
  ```

# Using zypper on OpenSUSE-based distributions

We can use `zypper` to install Kibana on OpenSUSE-based distributions using the following command:

```
sudo zypper install kibana
```

# Installing Kibana on Windows

Follow the steps to install Kibana on Windows:

2. From the Elastic download section (https://www.elastic.co/downloads/kibana), we can download the .zip windows archive for Kibana v6.x.

3. Create a folder called kibana-6.x-windows-x86_64 by unzipping the zipped archive; we refer to this folder path as $KIBANA_HOME. Now move to the $KIBANA_HOME directory by using the following expression:

```
cd c:\kibana-6.x-windows-x86_64
```

3. To start Kibana, we need to run the following command:

```
.\bin\kibana
```

# Beats

Beat is a separately-installable product; they are lightweight data shippers. There are many Beats available, as follows:

- Packetbeat
- Metricbeat
- Filebeat
- Winlogbeat
- Heartbeat

# Packetbeat

There are many ways to download and install Packetbeat, depending on your operating system. Let's see different commands for different types of OSes:

- **To install Packtbeat on deb use the following command**:

```
sudo apt-get install libpcap0.8
curl -L -O
https://artifacts.elastic.co/downloads/beats/packetbeat/packetbeat-
6.2.1-amd64.deb
sudo dpkg -i packetbeat-6.2.1-amd64.deb
```

- **To install Packetbeat on rpm use the following command**:

```
sudo yum install libpcap
curl -L -O
https://artifacts.elastic.co/downloads/beats/packetbeat/packetbeat-
6.x-x86_64.rpm
sudo rpm -vi packetbeat-6.2.1-x86_64.rpm
```

- **To install Packetbeat on macOS use the following command**:

```
curl -L -O
https://artifacts.elastic.co/downloads/beats/packetbeat/packetbeat-
6x-darwin-x86_64.tar.gz
tar xzvf packetbeat-6.2.1-darwin-x86_64.tar.gz
```

- **To install Packetbeat on the Windows environment, perform the following steps:**

1. Get the Packtebeat Windows zip file from the Elastic downloads section.
2. Extract the zip file to `C:\Program Files`.
3. Rename the extracted file Packetbeat.
4. Run the PowerShell prompt as an Administrator.
5. To install Packetbeat as a Windows service, run the following command:

```
PS > cd 'C:\Program Files\Packetbeat'
PS C:\Program Files\Packetbeat> .\install-service-packetbeat.ps1
```

# Metricbeat

There are different ways to install Metricbeat on your operating system. Using the following expressions, we can install Metricbeat on different OSes:

- **To install Metricbeat on deb use the following command**:

```
curl -L -O
https://artifacts.elastic.co/downloads/beats/metricbeat/metricbeat-
6.x-amd64.deb
sudo dpkg -i metricbeat-6.x-amd64.deb
```

- **To install Meticbeat on rpm use the following command**:

```
curl -L -O
https://artifacts.elastic.co/downloads/beats/metricbeat/metricbeat-
6.x-x86_64.rpm
sudo rpm -vi metricbeat-6.x-x86_64.rpm
```

- **To install Meticbeat on macOS use the following command**:

```
curl -L -O
https://artifacts.elastic.co/downloads/beats/metricbeat/metricbeat-
6.x-darwin-x86_64.tar.gz
tar xzvf metricbeat-6.x-darwin-x86_64.tar.gz
```

- **To install Meticbeat on Windows perform the following steps**:

1. Download the Metricbeat Windows zip from the Elastic download section.
2. Extract the file to the `C:\Program Files` directory.
3. Rename the **metricbeat** long directory name to Metricbeat.
4. Run the PowerShell prompt as an Administrator.

 If you're running Windows XP, you may need to download and install PowerShell.

1. Run the following commands to install Metricbeat as a Windows service:
2. To install Metricbeat, run the following commands from the PowerShell prompt:

```
PS > cd 'C:\Program Files\Metricbeat'
PS C:\Program Files\Metricbeat> .\install-service-metricbeat.ps1
```

# Filebeat

We can download and install Filebeat on different operating systems in the following ways:

- **To install Filebear on deb use the following command**:

```
curl -L -O
https://artifacts.elastic.co/downloads/beats/filebeat/filebeat-6.x-
amd64.deb
sudo dpkg -i filebeat-6.x-amd64.deb
```

- **To install Filebeat on rpm use the following command**:

```
curl -L -O
https://artifacts.elastic.co/downloads/beats/filebeat/filebeat-6.x-
x86_64.rpm
sudo rpm -vi filebeat-6.x-x86_64.rpm
```

- **To install Filebeat on macOS use the following command**:

```
curl -L -O
https://artifacts.elastic.co/downloads/beats/filebeat/filebeat-6.x-
darwin-x86_64.tar.gz
tar xzvf filebeat-6.2.1-darwin-x86_64.tar.gz
```

- **To install Filebeat on Windows perform the following steps**:

1. From the Elastic downloads section, download the **Filebeat Windows zip** file.
2. Extract the zip file into C:\Program Files.
3. Rename the long filebeat directory to **Filebeat**.
4. Open a PowerShell prompt as an administrator.
5. From the PowerShell prompt, execute the following commands:

```
PS > cd 'C:\Program Files\Filebeat'
PS C:\Program Files\Filebeat> .\install-service-filebeat.ps1
```

# Summary

In this chapter, we introduced you to Elastic Stack, where we discussed the different components of Elastic Stack, such as Elasticsearch, Logstash, Kibana, and different Beats. Then we looked at different use cases of Elastic Stack, such as System Performance Monitoring, where we monitor the system's performance, Log Management, where we collect different logs and monitor them from a central place, and Application Performance Monitoring, where we monitor our application by connecting it to a central APM server. We also covered Application Data Analysis, where we analyze the application's data, Security Monitoring and Alerting, where we secure our stack using X-Pack, monitor it regularly, and configure alerts to keep an eye on changes that can impact the system's performance, and Data Visualization, where we use Kibana to create different types of visualizations using the available data.

In the next chapter, we'll cover different methods of pushing data into Kibana, such as from RDBMS, files, system metrics, CSV, and applications. We'll start with different Beats to demonstrate the complete process of configuring these Beats and sending data directly to Elasticsearch or via Logstash to Elasticsearch. Then, we'll look at how to import data from CSV by configuring Logstash to take input and insert data into Elasticsearch. After CSV, we'll fetch data from RDBMS using SQL queries through the JDBC plugin and insert it into Elasticsearch. We'll use the preceding methods to insert data into Elasticsearch, and then we'll configure Kibana to fetch the data by creating an index pattern. In this way, we can fetch any type of data into Kibana and can then perform different operations on that data.

# 2
# Getting Data into Kibana

In this chapter, we'll cover different methods to push data into Kibana, such as from RDBMS, from different files, from system metrics, using CSV files, and from different applications. We'll start with different Beats, such as Packetbeat, Metricbeat, and Filebeat, to demonstrate the complete process, from configuring these Beats and then sending data from Beats to Elasticsearch or Logstash. Then we'll look at how to import data from CSV by configuring Logstash to take input and insert data into Elasticsearch. After CSV we'll fetch data from RDBMS using SQL queries through the JDBC plugin and insert it into Elasticsearch. For all these methods, we're inserting data into Elasticsearch. Once the data is inserted into Elasticsearch, we can configure Kibana to fetch the Elasticsearch data by creating an index pattern. In this way, we can fetch any type of data into Kibana and can perform different operations on that data.

In this chapter we are going to cover the following topics:

- **Difference between Beats and Logstash**: We will cover how these two are different in their functioning
- **Configuring Beats to get data**: Here we will cover how different beats can be configured to fetch the data and send to Elasticsearch Cluster
- **Configuring Logstash to get data**: Under this section, we will cover Logstash configuration to get data and push that into Elasticsearch Cluster
  - **Configuring Logstash to read CSV data**: Here we will configure Logstash to read CSV data
  - **Configuring Logstash to read RDBMS data**: Here we will configure Logstash to fetch data from MySQL
- **Configuring index patterns in Kibana**: We will use index patterns to show Elasticsearch index data in Kibana

# Difference between Beats and Logstash

Beats are basically lightweight data shippers that are designed for a specific purpose, while Logstash is more generic and can be configured for multiple use cases. Beats have a smaller footprint, while Logstash has a larger footprint. We have different Beats for different purposes, such as Filebeat for handling files, Metricbeat for capturing system metrics, Packetbeat to capture network packet data, while Logstash has different plugins for input, filter, and output. We can read CSV data, RDBMS data, Beat data, or any other third-party application's data in Logstash, and after transformation can be sent to multiple sources. So basically, if we want to do any sort of data processing or want to capture any complex data, which isn't possible using Beats, we must use Logstash. If we just want to read log data, system metrics data, or any data that's easily available using Beats, we should go for Beats in that case.

# Configuring Beats to get data

Here, we'll cover how to configure different Beats to get data, such as using Filebeat to capture file data, Metricbeat to capture system metrics data, and Metricbeat to capture network packet data. Using Beats in this way means we can start getting data, as these Beats are installed on a machine from where we want to capture the data, and once they're configured, they allow you to capture the data from the machine and send it to an Elasticsearch cluster directly or via Logstash. Beats are basically lightweight data shippers built for a specific purpose. There are different types of Beats, such as Packetbeat, Filebeat, Metricbeat, Auditbeat, Heartbeat, and Winlogbeat. The following diagram shows how these Beats are sending data to a central Elasticsearch Cluster:

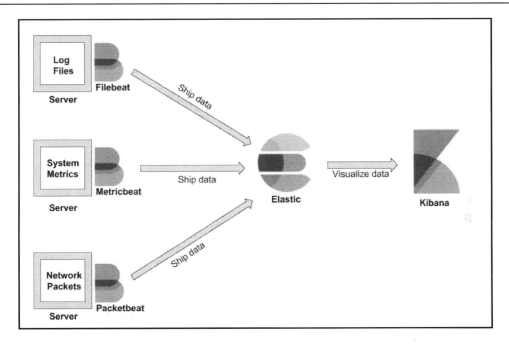

In the preceding diagram, we have Filebeat, which is reading log data from /var/log, then we have Metricbeat which reads system metric data, such as memory usage and CPU usage, and then we have Packetbeat which reads network packet data on the server. This way, we can configure the Beats and get continuous data from them into our central Elasticsearch cluster. Now let's configure them to understand how we can get data from different Beats.

# Filebeat

Filebeat is a lightweight data shipper that forwards the log data from different servers to a central place where we can analyze that log data. We can install them on any server from where we want to capture the file data, such as Apache log or any application log. In Filebeat, we have different options, such as configuring the input, output, and modules. Using the input option, we can configure from where we want to read the data, for example the /var/log directory.

Let's see the input screenshot under the `filebeat.yml` file:

```
#============================ Filebeat inputs ============================

filebeat.inputs:

# Each - is an input. Most options can be set at the input level, so
# you can use different inputs for various configurations.
# Below are the input specific configurations.

- type: log

  # Change to true to enable this input configuration.
  enabled: false

  # Paths that should be crawled and fetched. Glob based paths.
  paths:
    - /var/log/*.log
    - /home/user/workplace/kfc/*.log
    #- c:\programdata\elasticsearch\logs\*

  # Exclude lines. A list of regular expressions to match. It drops the lines that are
  # matching any regular expression from the list.
  #exclude_lines: ['^DBG']

  # Include lines. A list of regular expressions to match. It exports the lines that are
  # matching any regular expression from the list.
  #include_lines: ['^ERR', '^WARN']

  # Exclude files. A list of regular expressions to match. Filebeat drops the files that
  # are matching any regular expression from the list. By default, no files are dropped.
  #exclude_files: ['.gz$']

  # Optional additional fields. These fields can be freely picked
  # to add additional information to the crawled log files for filtering
  #fields:
  #   level: debug
  #   review: 1
```

In the preceding screenshot, you can see the configuration option provided in the `filebeat.yml` file. We can configure any directory from where Filebeat will start reading the data. Using the module block, we can configure different modules as per our requirement. We can use the dashboard section in Filebeat to configure ready-made dashboards. They're very handy as they save a lot of time when creating different visualizations and then integrating them for creating dashboards. Under the output block, we can configure the Filebeat data output, such as where we want to push the Filebeat data, such as Elasticsearch or Logstash. Let's see the screenshot of the output section under the `filebeat.yml` file:

```
#========================== Outputs ==========================

# Configure what output to use when sending the data collected by the beat.

#-------------------------- Elasticsearch output --------------------------
output.elasticsearch:
  # Array of hosts to connect to.
  hosts: ["localhost:9200"]

  # Optional protocol and basic auth credentials.
  #protocol: "https"
  #username: "elastic"
  #password: "changeme"

#-------------------------- Logstash output --------------------------
#output.logstash:
  # The Logstash hosts
  #hosts: ["localhost:5044"]

  # Optional SSL. By default is off.
  # List of root certificates for HTTPS server verifications
  #ssl.certificate_authorities: ["/etc/pki/root/ca.pem"]

  # Certificate for SSL client authentication
  #ssl.certificate: "/etc/pki/client/cert.pem"

  # Client Certificate Key
  #ssl.key: "/etc/pki/client/cert.key"
```

In the preceding screenshot, we have output section, where we can see two options: the Elasticsearch output and the Logstash output. We can configure them as per our requirements, such as providing the Elasticsearch cluster credentials in case we want to push Filebeat data directly into Elasticsearch, or configuring the Logstash output if we want to send Filebeat data first to Logstash for further modification, or updating and then moving the Logstash-modified data into Elasticsearch. If we want to send Filebeat data directly into Elasticsearch, we can add the following expression for Elasticsearch output in the filebeat.yml file:

```
output.elasticsearch:
  hosts: ["https://localhost:9200"]
  username: "elastic_username"
  password: "elastic_password"
  index: "filebeat-%{[beat.version]}-%{+yyyy.MM.dd}"
  ssl.certificate_authorities: ["/etc/pki/root/ca.pem"]
  ssl.certificate: "/etc/pki/client/cert.pem"
  ssl.key: "/etc/pki/client/cert.key"
```

Using the preceding `output.elasticsearch` section, we can configure Filebeat to send data to the Elasticsearch cluster. We need to provide the username and password only if our Elasticsearch cluster is password-protected. Certificate details are required in case the Elastic stack is secured with SSL. In this way, we have the flexibility to use any device. Filebeat is used when we want to fetch the data from different files, such as system log files, application log files, or custom files.

# Packetbeat

Monitoring is very important to know about what's going on as, when we develop an application, we assume that it will work as per the given use case, but sometimes it stops working and suddenly we have to debug the application to get the root cause of the application outage. Here, we're following a reactive approach where we wait for any bug and then waste our time debugging and fixing the application issue. Another approach is the proactive approach. After developing the application we use to deploy it along with monitoring where we can check different aspects, such as the system, network, application, or database.

This monitoring may take some additional time in the beginning, but can do the miracles for us as this can alert us about any possible bugs or any required system upgrades. Packetbeat provides the packet-related information, using which we can get better insight into any issue. We can configure Packetbeat by modifying the `packetbeat.yml` file. In this file, we have the option to configure input, output, modules, and different ports that we can handle. Although we can get a sufficient amount of network information using Packetbeat, if we want more detailed packet-analysis data, we can use Wireshark's CLI tool, tshark.

 TShark is basically a command-line version of Wireshark that's designed to capture and display network packets.

We can configure Packetbeat to send network packet data by doing configuration changes in the `packetbeat.yml` file. On Ubuntu, the `packetbeat.yml` file can be found under the `/etc/packetbeat/` location. For sniffing data, we can configure different network devices on the `packetbeat.yml` file. This can be done as show below:

```
#============================== Network device
==============================
packetbeat.interfaces.device: any
```

In the preceding expression, we have given any for the interface device, which means we want to sniff all interfaces that are connected. Then, under transaction protocols, we can select the protocol on which we want to sniff, such as ICMP, DNS, or HTTP. We need to provide different ports as well:

```
#=========================== Transaction protocols
===========================
packetbeat.protocols:
- type: icmp
  # Enable ICMPv4 and ICMPv6 monitoring. Default: false
  enabled: true

- type: amqp
  # Configure the ports where to listen for AMQP traffic. You can disable
  # the AMQP protocol by commenting out the list of ports.
  ports: [5672]

- type: cassandra
  #Cassandra port for traffic monitoring.
  ports: [9042]

- type: dns
  # Configure the ports where to listen for DNS traffic. You can disable
  # the DNS protocol by commenting out the list of ports.
  ports: [53]

  # include_authorities controls whether or not the dns.authorities field
  # (authority resource records) is added to messages.
  include_authorities: true

  # include_additionals controls whether or not the dns.additionals field
  # (additional resource records) is added to messages.
  include_additionals: true

- type: http
  # Configure the ports where to listen for HTTP traffic. You can disable
  # the HTTP protocol by commenting out the list of ports.
  ports: [80, 8080, 8000, 5000, 8002]

- type: memcache
  # Configure the ports where to listen for memcache traffic. You can
disable
  # the Memcache protocol by commenting out the list of ports.
  ports: [11211]
  . . . . . . .
  . . . . . . .
```

In the preceding transaction protocol ports, we can change the port numbers in case default ports aren't used. By just commenting the list of ports from the Packetbeat configuration file, we can disable that protocol. We have the option to create a preconfigured Packetbeat dashboard in Kibana by just providing the Kibana endpoint in the Packetbeat configuration file. If Elasticsearch is hosted on a cloud platform, we need to provide the cloud ID of Elasticsearch.

Under the output, we need to provide the credentials of Elasticsearch and Logstash, using which Packetbeat data can be sent to these servers. For the Elasticsearch output configuration, we have to provide the hostname, protocol, username, password, and so on. The Elasticsearch output credentials are required if we want to push Packetbeat data directly into Elasticsearch. For Logstash output configuration, we need to provide the hostname and SSL certificate details in case we have configured SSL. We can configure Logstash if we want to modify or add additional fields before pushing Packetbeat data into Elasticsearch. We can also customize logging by changing the log level, also we can customize it to log only certain components. X-Pack monitoring can also be enabled from this configuration file to get Packetbeat monitoring details on the X-Pack monitoring screen:

```
#===================== Outputs =========================
# Configure what output to use when sending the data collected by the beat.

#-------------------- Elasticsearch output --------------------
output.elasticsearch:
  # Array of hosts to connect to.
  hosts: ["localhost:9200"]

  # Optional protocol and basic auth credentials.
  #protocol: "https"
  #username: "elastic"
  #password: "changeme"

#-------------------- Logstash output --------------------
#output.logstash:
  # The Logstash hosts
  #hosts: ["localhost:5044"]

  # Optional SSL. By default is off.
  # List of root certificates for HTTPS server verifications
  #ssl.certificate_authorities: ["/etc/pki/root/ca.pem"]

  # Certificate for SSL client authentication
  #ssl.certificate: "/etc/pki/client/cert.pem"

  # Client Certificate Key
  #ssl.key: "/etc/pki/client/cert.key"

#===================== Logging =========================

# Sets log level. The default log level is info.
# Available log levels are: error, warning, info, debug
#logging.level: debug

# At debug level, you can selectively enable logging only for some components.
# To enable all selectors use ["*"]. Examples of other selectors are "beat",
# "publish", "service".
#logging.selectors: ["*"]
```

In the preceding screenshot, we can see the Elasticsearch output, Logstash output, and Logging section with the available configuration options, which we can change per our requirements. After configuring the Packetbeat configuration file, we can start getting network packet details into Elasticsearch directly or through Logstash. We can verify the Packetbeat data into Elasticsearch by listing all indices and checking the index with a name, such as `packetbeat-6.x.x-2019.xx.xx`. Packetbeat installation is covered in the previous chapter so you can refer to that. Once installation is done, you can modify the configuration file and restart packetbeat to get the data into Elasticsearch, from where we can get the data into Kibana by creating the index pattern. Once data is in Kibana, we can analyze it or create a dashboard using visualizations. Now let's see how we can configure Metricbeat to get system metrics from a remote server.

# Metricbeat

Metricbeat is a lightweight data shipper that sits on a remote machine and sends system metrics, such as CPU, memory, Disk IO, network IO, and running processes. This information is quite helpful as we should know about the system metrics of the server on which we're hosting our application, because if there's any issue on the system, it will impact the application. Metricbeat helps us to fetch metrics from the system and different services running on that server, such as Nginx, Apache, MySQL, PostgreSQL, MongoDB, and Redis.

Metricbeat has different internal modules that can be configured to collect metrics from different services, such as Nginx, Apache, MySQL, MongoDB, and PostgreSQL. We just need to enable the modules per our requirement and it starts receiving data from the configured modules. Beats ensure the data flow, and won't skip any data even if there are network issues. In case of a network outage or any other issue, Metricbeat holds the data and sends it back to Elasticsearch or Logstash.

After installing Metricbeat, we can open and modify the `metricbeat.yml` configuration file per our requirements. In the `metricbeat.yml` file, we have different options, such as the module-configuration section, through which we can enable the modules, then we have dashboards section, using which we can enable the dashboard for Metricbeat in Kibana. From Beats version 6.0.0 onward, we can load Metricbeat dashboards using the Kibana API by providing the Kibana setup details, such as hosts. If our Elasticsearch is hosted on the cloud, we can add the cloud ID of Elasticsearch under the Elastic Cloud section in the `metricbeat.yml` file.

Finally, we have to provide the Elasticsearch and Logstash output details that Metricbeat uses to send the data. In the Elasticsearch output configuration, we have to provide the **host name**, **protocol**, **username**, **password**, and so on. After Elasticsearch, we have the Logstash output section, where we have to provide some details, such as the host name, and SSL details in case SSL is enabled on the Logstash setup. Then we have a logging section, through which we can configure the debug level of logging, and then selectors, using which we can enable certain components only. Then we have the Xpack monitoring flag. which can be enabled from the `xpack.monitoring.enabled` option. Once enabled, it can be seen on the X-Pack monitoring screen. The configuration of Metricbeat is quite similar to other Beats, such as Packetbeat and Filebeat.

# Configuring Logstash to get data

In the previous section, we covered how to get data in Elasticsearch using different Beats. They're easy to install, configure, and then you can start receiving data from the server. Sometimes we need to do more than just configure a specific, single-purpose Beats that sits on the server and sends data to an Elasticsearch cluster and for the Logstash that's there. Logstash is a data pipeline we can use to configure input to take data from multiple types of data sources, such as files, databases, CSV, or Kafka, and after taking the input, we can configure the output to send data on different sources, such as files, databases, Kafka, or Elasticsearch. Another important feature of Logstash is **filter**, using which we can transform the input data before sending it to the output. Let's check out a Logstash configuration format:

```
input
{
 file
 {
 path => "/var/log/apache.log"
 type => "apache-access"
 start_position => "beginning"
 }
}
filter
{
 grok
 { match => [ "message", "%{COMBINEDAPACHELOG}" ] }
}
output
{
  elasticsearch
  {
 hosts => ["localhost:9200"]
```

```
    }
  }
```

In the preceding expression, we have three sections. The first is the input section, where we're reading the Apache access log data using a file plugin, a type is there to tell Logstash that it's Apache access data, while `start_position` is there to configure it to read data from the beginning of the file. The second is the filter section, where we're applying a grok pattern on the Apache log in order to extract each field from the message parameter of the log file. The third is the output section, which is configured to send data into the Elasticsearch cluster. Now let's see how we can read data from different sources, such as CSV data or RDBMS data, by configuring Logstash.

# Configuring Logstash to read CSV data

When you have data in the form of a CSV file and you want to push that data into Elasticsearch, you can use Logstash as it can be configured to read your CSV data directly from a file and push it to Elasticsearch. We need to modify the Logstash configuration file to take CSV data as input. If we want to analyze or visualize data in Kibana, our data should exist in Elasticsearch, from where you can use it in Kibana. CSV data is the data source that's easily available on different sources. If you want to fetch any government data, the data can easily be downloaded in CSV format from their websites. The size of the CSV file is often quite large and you can't easily explore your data in CSV format.

Let's say you've downloaded a CSV data from anywhere; you can take the example of **Crimes – 2001 to present** data from the `data.gov` website. On this website, we can freely download multiple data sources in CSV format. Once you download any CSV file or create your own, you need to know how to push this data into Elasticsearch so that you can apply data analytics and visualize the data using Kibana. So let's start the process and learn how we can configure Logstash to send the CSV data into an Elasticsearch cluster after reading it from a file. You need to do following (here I am taking the example of the crimes dataset from the data.gov website):

1.  Download a CSV file (for example, `crimes_2001.csv`) from the `data.gov` website (`https://catalog.data.gov/dataset?res_format=CSV`). We have different fields, such as **ID, Case Number, Date, Block, IUCR, Primary Type, Description, Location, Description, Arrest, Domestic, Beat, District, Ward, Community Area, FBI Code, X Coordinate, Y Coordinate, Year, Updated On, Latitude, Longitude**, and **Location**, in this CSV file.

You can download this CSV file from this book's Github link:
`https://github.com/PacktPublishing/Kibana-7-Quick-Start-Guide/`
`blob/master/Chapter02/crimes_2001.csv.`

2. Create a Logstash configuration file, using which we can read the CSV data and write it to the Elasticsearch cluster. In our Logstash configuration file, we need to write the following expression (for example `crimes.conf`):

```
input {
    file {
        path => "/home/anurag/crimes_2001.csv"
        start_position => beginning
    }
}
filter {
    csv {
        columns => [
                "ID",
                "Case Number",
                "Date",
                "Block",
                "IUCR",
                "Primary Type",
                "Description",
                "Location Description",
                "Arrest",
                "Domestic",
                "Beat",
                "District",
                "Ward",
                "Community Area",
                "FBI Code",
                "X Coordinate",
                "Y Coordinate",
                "Year",
                "Updated On",
                "Latitude",
                "Longitude",
                "Location"
        ]
        separator => ","
        }
}
output {
    elasticsearch {
        action => "index"
```

```
hosts => ["127.0.0.1:9200"]
index => "crimes"
    }
}
```

 You can download this Logstash configuration from this book's Github link:
https://github.com/PacktPublishing/Kibana-7-Quick-Start-Guide/blob/master/Chapter02/crimes.conf.

3. To execute the Logstash configuration file, run the following command:

   **/usr/share/logstash/bin/logstash —f
   /etc/logstash/conf.d/crimes.conf**

4. You can verify the **crimes** index in Elasticsearch by listing all indices in the browser:

   **http://localhost:9200/_cat/indices?v**

5. If your index is listed, that means your data is successfully inserted into Elasticsearch Cluster. You can see your index data in Elasticsearch using the following expression:

   **http://localhost:9200/crimes/_search?pretty**

In this way, using the Logstash file input plugin and the CSV filter plugin, you can push any CSV data into Elasticsearch. Once data is inserted, you can perform the search and analytics, and create dashboards.

# Configuring Logstash to read RDBMS data

In the previous section, we configured Logstash to read CSV data from a file, but you can also configure it to read RBMS data using SQL queries directly. Let's take the example of a MySQL database and see how we can configure the JDBC plugin of Logstash to fetch the data by running SQL queries on your RDBMS. Before configuring Logstash, we need to download the JDBC jar file and configure the JDBC input plugin, using which we configure the Logstash JDBC input plugin so that it connects with the MySQL database. Using this plugin, we can execute SQL queries to get the records from the database.

After a successful connection, Logstash can push the obtained records to Elastic Cluster:

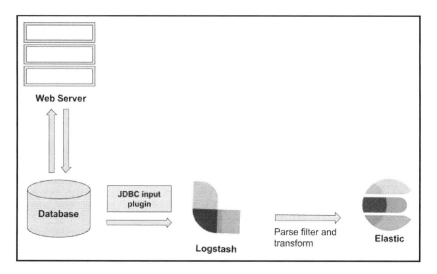

Web server pushing the data to database

The preceding diagram shows the flow where the web server pushes the data to a database and we obtain it using the JDBC input plugin of Logstash. When the parsing is complete, this data is pushed to Elasticsearch.

After pushing the MySQL data into Elasticsearch by executing the SQL queries using the JDBC input plugin, we can create index pattern in Kibana to make the dashboards. To fetch the MySQL data into Elasticsearch, we configure Logstash by creating a configuration file in /etc/logstash/conf.d directory. Now let's see how we can do that by creating the configuration file as teams.conf and then writing the following expression:

```
input {
 jdbc {
    jdbc_driver_library => "/usr/share/logstash/mysql-connector-
java-5.1.23-bin.jar"
    jdbc_driver_class => "com.mysql.jdbc.Driver"
    #jdbc connection string for connecting to the MySQL database
    jdbc_connection_string => "jdbc:mysql://url-of-db:3306
/db_name?zeroDateTimeBehavior=convertToNull"
    # username and password of MySQL server
    jdbc_user => "username"
    jdbc_password => "password"
    # Schedule this process at a regular interval, here we are
running every minute.
    schedule => "* * * * *"
```

```
        # query to return blog details
        statement => "select t.name as team, t.description, p.name as
player, p.about as       about from team as t left join player as p
on t.id = p.team_id where p.id >             :sql_last_value"
        use_column_value => true
        tracking_column => id
        tracking_column_type => "numeric"
      }
  }
  output {
    elasticsearch {
        hosts => "http://127.0.0.1:9200"
        index => "teams"
        }
  }
```

In the preceding expression of the Logstash configuration file, we have two sections. The first is input, where we connect to the MySQL database to get the data by executing the SQL queries using the JDBC plugin of Logstash. Then we have the output section, which uses the elasticsearch plugin under output to send the fetched data into the Elasticsearch cluster. Logstash doesn't include the JDBC plugin out of the box, so we need to configure it by downloading the JDBC driver library file: `mysql-connector-java-5.1.23-bin.jar`.

We can provide the path in `jdbc_driver_library` under the input section of the Logstash configuration file after the library file is downloaded. We then have to provide the driver class for the `dbc_driver_class` parameter under the JDBC driver library, then we'll create the connection string to connect the database. There are a few things that we need to provide in the connection string, such as are DB type, URL of the database, port of database, database name, and, after the connection string, we need to provide the MySQL username and password.

 You can download the DB dump from this book's Github link:
https://github.com/PacktPublishing/Kibana-7-Quick-Start-Guide/
blob/master/Chapter02/team_db.sql.

We can configure the job scheduler to execute the Logstash configuration on a regular interval, after configuring the MySQL database connection. For a schedule, we need to provide the pattern, such as when we want to execute the scheduler, be it every minute, every hour, every day at 4 pm, or every Monday at noon. You can schedule the Logstash job per your requirements. The following expressions show how to create schedulers:

```
"* * * * * " => runs every second
"30 2 * * *" => runs as 2:30AM
"10 22 * * *" => runs at 10:10PM
```

After the scheduler, we have statement parameter where we need to provide the actual query which wants to execute on MySQL server. As we want to execute the query on regular interval, but only to fetch the incremental records once we've fetched some records, there's an option in the Logstash JDBC plugin to store the last value of any given field. We can achieve this by using `sql_last_value` in the query.

We then have `tracking_column`, which is used to provide the column name for `sql_last_value`. When we run this Logstash configuration for the first time, it will get all the records and set the value of the last ID in the file, which is stored in your home directory. When you execute this query again, the last ID will be replaced with `sql_last_value`. Along with the name of the tracking column, we will also need to provide the data type of the column we're tracking. In our case, this field is numeric. Execute the Logstash configuration file using the following command on Ubuntu once the changes are done:

```
/usr/share/logstash/bin/logstash -f /etc/logstash/conf.d/teams.conf
```

The scheduler can execute the expression per the scheduler expression. We can also add this expression under the cron entry to autostart the Logstash configuration execution whenever the system restarts. To open the crontab entry in Linux, run following command:

```
crontab -e
```

We can open or edit the crontab file in the Linux system by executing the preceding command. To make sure that after every machine-restart Logstash configuration file execution starts automatically, execute the preceding command. Once executed, we can start executing SQL queries to get the data from the MySQL database without any manual intervention:

```
@reboot /usr/share/logstash/bin/logstash -f /etc/logstash/conf.d/teams.conf
```

In the preceding crontab expression, we have written `@reboot`, which ensures that whenever the system is restarted for any reason, it will start executing the Logstash configuration file. In this section, we covered how the Logstash JDBC plugin can be configured to fetch MySQL DB data and then push it into the Elasticsearch cluster.

# Configuring index patterns in Kibana

So far, we've covered how to push data into Elasticsearch from different sources, such as Beats and Logstash. Once the data is pushed into your Elasticsearch cluster, you can get that into Kibana by creating the index pattern. So the ultimate aim of Elastic Stack is to get data, analyze it, visualize it, and extract meaningful information – for that, we can fetch data from different sources, push them to a central Elasticsearch cluster, make them available to Kibana using index patterns, and analyze them.

Let's check how the index pattern can be created in Kibana to access Elasticsearch index data. Click on the **Management** link from the left menu to open the **Management** page. This will show you Elasticsearch and the Kibana block; under the Kibana block, click on the **Index Pattern** link to open the index pattern page. The following screenshot shows the index pattern page:

In the preceding screenshot, we can see the default index pattern, such as **apm**. On this page, we have a **Create Index Pattern** button on the top-left corner, click on it. This will open the following screen:

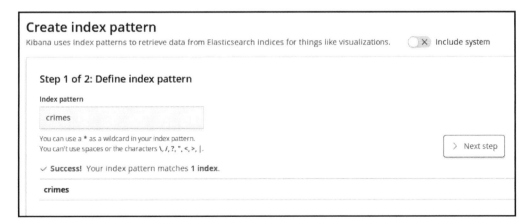

The preceding screenshot shows the **Create index pattern** page where we need to provide the name of the Elasticsearch index. Once we start typing the name, Kibana will show the suggested name – after typing the correct name, click on the **Next step** button to move to the next step. Here's step 2:

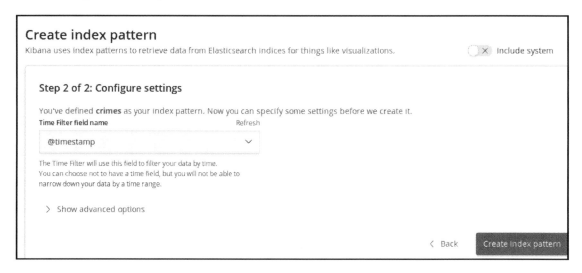

The preceding screenshot shows us the second step of index-pattern creation, where we need to select the time filter field name. Click on the **Create index pattern** button after selecting the field from the dropdown. You can see the following screen once the index pattern is created in Kibana:

In the preceding screenshot, you can see the field names with their type, format, searchable, aggregatable, and excluded options. We can also edit the field, date format, and so on. Once we are happy with the fields and their formats, we can explore the data under the Discover option of Kibana.

To discover the data, we need to click on the **Discover** link from the left menu of Kibana, which will open the following screen of data display:

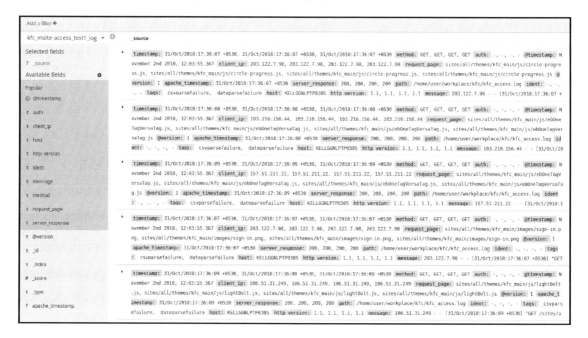

In the preceding screenshot, we can see the actual data, which is listed as the **_source** column. On the left side, we have two options: **Selected fields**, where we can see the fields that are selected to display, and **Available fields**, where we have the option to add fields by clicking on the add button by hovering on the field. This way, we can customize the data view. We can also query this data, filter it, and apply time-based filters. These options are available for us under data discover, which we are going to cover in next chapter.

# Summary

In this chapter, we looked at how to get data from different sources into Kibana, and then perform data analytics and visualization on it. We covered different ways to get data in Elasticsearch. We saw how Beats, a lightweight data shipper, can be installed on a server to send data. Under Beats, we covered Filebeat, which reads file data, such as Apache logs, system logs, and application logs, and can send them to Elasticsearch directly or using Logstash. Then we configured Metricbeat to read system metrics, such as CPU usage, memory usage, MySQL metrics, and then Packetbeat, using which we can read network packet data to get insights from it.

We covered how Logstash can be used to get data and apply filters before sending it to Elasticsearch. In the first section, we covered how to fetch CSV data using Logstash, where we passed a CSV file as input and specified the columns to send the data to Elasticsearch. After that, we covered how to configure the JDBC plugin to fetch MySQL data by running the SQL statement and applying the tracking column, using which the incremental data can be fetched in Logstash. Once the MySQL data was read, it was pushed to Elasticsearch for analysis. Using Beats and Logstash, we can push data into Elasticsearch, but to analyze and visualize the data, we need this data in Kibana and for that, we have to create an index pattern in Kibana. Once the index pattern is created, we can see the data under the Discover option of Kibana, where we can apply a filter, run queries, and select fields to display.

In the next chapter, we'll cover how we can explore this data in Kibana, which is fetched from different sources and stored in the Elasticsearch cluster. We'll see how we can query, data filter, time filter, and drill down further to get the required dataset for analysis.

# 3
# Exploring Data

In this chapter, we'll learn how to play with data and get the desired information by exploring it. In Kibana, we have the **Discover** tab, which provides you with features to explore your data. We can do many things under **Discover**, such as limit the number of field displays to focus on what you want to see. Say you're only interested in few columns; you can add only them in your data display. You can filter your data using the Elasticsearch data filter; it offers a handy option where you can directly apply the filter on your data. Apart from the data filter, we can apply a time-based filter. Let's say we want to see the data of last week only; this can easily be filtered using the time-based filter. Then, we have the Elasticsearch query language, which can be directly applied using the intuitive interface of Kibana, so we can run a very simple query or a complex query. The best part is that we can apply all of these in a single instance to explore what exactly we want to see. For an example, say there was an issue in one of my systems last week that was related to Apache and we were getting a 500 HTTP code, how can we find the root cause of the issue? We can break our problem statement into different requirements where you can to see the data of last week, an index should display the Apache log data, need to apply a filter with HTTP code 500, and so on. In Kibana Discover, we can do all of this with the click of some buttons and by filling in some values only. In this chapter, we're going to cover all of these options and how this is going to help us in exploring our data.

In this chapter, we are going to cover the following topics:

- **Discovering your data:** Under this, we are going to learn how Kibana Discover can be utilized to discover your data
    - **Limiting your field display:** Here, we will see how to limit the filed display for viewing your data
    - **Expanded view of the data:** Here, we will cover how to expand the document to see all of its fields

- **Dissecting your data:** Under this section, we will cover different **Discover** options such as query data, filter on fields, and time
  - **The time filter:** We will see how to apply a time-based filter on your data
  - **Using the search bar to search your data:** We will cover how to search using the search box
  - **Filtering your data:** How a data filter can be applied on your dataset
- **Saving your filtered data:** Here, we will cover how to save these search results and export them for future use
  - **Saving your search:** How to save the search result
  - **Managing saved searches:** How to export the saved search result

# Discover your data

Once you have created the index pattern in Kibana, your Elasticsearch data can be accessed from Kibana directly. So once the data is available, we can explore it using the different options of Kibana Discover. The following screen appears when we first click on **Discover** from the left menu in Kibana:

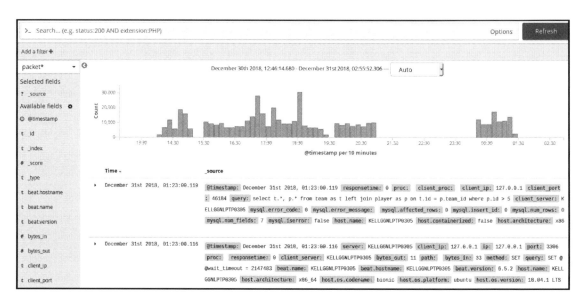

In the preceding screenshot, you can see the histogram, which shows the date against the timestamp when the records get added. It shows **@timestamp per day** on the x axis and **Count** on the y axis. Under the histogram, we have the actual data, which is shown with **Time** and the **_source** field. There are different things we can do here to see the specific fields of records, records with a specific time range, expanded with of one document to show field, and values in a tabular view. Now let's see how we can use some of these features.

# Limit Your Field Display

By default, **Discover** shows **Time** and the **_source** field, where time is sorted in descending order while **_source** contains all fields and their values. This view isn't very good if we want to play around with certain fields rather than the complete set of fields. We can limit the fields displayed by adding only those fields that we want to see and removing the fields we don't need. On the left side of the page, we have two options:

- **Selected fields:** It shows us the fields that are added in the list, and we can see the values of these fields from the document display. We can remove fields by clicking on the **remove** button when hovering over the field name, if the field has been added from the *available fields* section.
- **Available fields:** This section shows the fields that are available and can be added to the data display. See the following screenshot where we have added some fields:

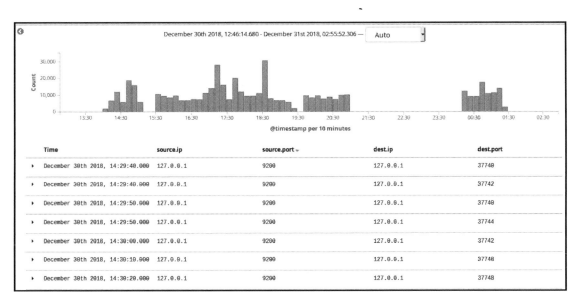

In the preceding screenshot, I have added only destination IP, destination port, source IP, and source port. This has created a nice view, using which we can easily drill down into the data to get only the desired fields. As I have the desired fields, any further drilling down can be done using a query or filter, which we'll see in future sections of this chapter.

# Expanded View of the Data

From a complete dataset, we can expand any document to get the field details, and other details as well. To check the expanded data view, we need to click on the **expand** button in front of each document. Once we click on this button, the data is expanded and we can see the complete field details, as follows:

In the preceding screenshot, we can see the expanded view of a single document; by clicking on the **expand** button, we can get this view. In this view, we can see all fields and their values in a tabular view with the option to filter in and out using any field value. Apart from the tabular view, we can also convert it to a **JSON** view by clicking the **JSON** tab next to the table tab at the top of the records view. We can see the surrounding documents of the document by clicking on the **View surrounding documents** button. We can also click on the **View single document** button to open the single document view, where we can see the data in tabular form or in **JSON** form.

# Dissect Your Data

To take a deep dive into our data, we need to explore and dissect it as per the requirement in hand. Kibana is quite useful for this data exploration as we have multiple options available to dissect the data; for example, on a single dataset we can do following:

- The time filter can be applied to filter the data on the basis of date and time
- A direct query can be applied to data using a query bar, such as `field: value`
- Filter your data using the interactive filter option
- Limit the number of fields you want to see

We have multiple options available, so let's explore them one by one.

# The time Filter

The time filter applies a time-based filter on your data and provides us with multiple ways to filter the time range. To set the time filter, we can use the **Time Picker**, which is available in the top-right corner of the page. There are different use cases where we can directly use the time filter on our data, such as if you need to focus on last-quarter data, or want to know what went wrong last week, or why the website went down at Christmas. We can use time picker to filter our data according to our requirements. There are different options in the Kibana time filter, such as quick time filter, relative time filter, absolute time filter, and recent time filter—let's see each of them in detail.

# The Quick Time Range Filter

Use the quick time range filter when you want to filter by **Today**, **This week**, **This month**, **This year**, **Last 15 min**, **Last 6 months**, **Last 5 years**, and so on. This type of time range filter is quite handy as we can directly click on a link and that's it; the filter is applied like if you have to apply a time filter for this week means you need to provide a range by providing start date and end date then your data would be filtered but in quick time range you just need to click on **This week** link and your filter is applied directly. The following screenshot shows the quick time range filter:

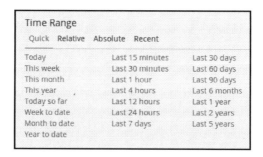

We can see some quick options, such as **Today**, **This week**, and **This year**. By clicking on the link, the time range can be applied on your data.

# The Relative Time Range Filter

The relative filter is an option using which we can set the from and to the range like from 15 minutes ago to 5 seconds ago, or from 1 year ago to 6 months ago and so on. The following screenshot shows the Relative time range filter screen:

In the preceding screenshot, we have two sections: **From** and **To**. In any section, we have a textbox to input the count and a dropdown to pick the required range, such as seconds ago, minutes ago, hours ago, seconds from now, or days from now. If you want to see the data from the last 15 minutes to the last 30 minutes, in the first textbox you need to type 30, then select **Minutes ago** from the dropdown; this will set the **From** to 30 minutes ago. Now, type 15 in the **To** textbox and select **Minutes ago** from the dropdown; this will set the end time to 15 minutes ago, so we'll be able to see the data between the last 15 to 30 minutes.

## The Absolute Time Range Filter

Using the absolute time filter, we can set the **From** and **To** range in an absolute way by selecting the exact data time using the calendar picker. This is the time range filter where we have to explicitly select the exact start-date time and end-date time to filter the data. The following screenshot shows the **Absolute** time filter:

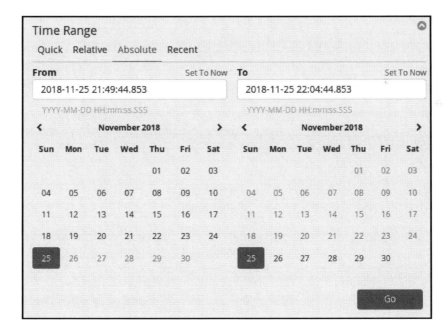

Here, we have the textbox, where we can input the date time in **YYYY-MM-DD HH:mm:ss SSS** format; for the date part, we have the calendar picker, from which we can select year, month, and then date, but time has to be explicitly added in the text box as there's no time picker.

## The Recent Time Range Filter

The Recent time filter shows the recent time ranges applied so that the user can go there directly and click on their recent time range choices. The following screenshot shows the Recent time range filter page:

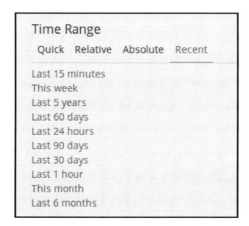

In the preceding screenshot, we can see only the links that we've already applied on our data. This is handy if we're playing with a certain fixed time range regularly. After setting the desired date range, we can move it backward or forward by clicking on the previous and next buttons on the left and right of the **Time Picker**. In this way, we can filter our data by any date range.

# Search bar to search your data

A search bar is used to search your data; it provides us with the option to join multiple queries with `and` or `or`. We have the options link in the search text box, using which we can enable autocomplete and simple syntax features. These autocomplete and simple syntax features help us to write the search criteria. See the following screenshot:

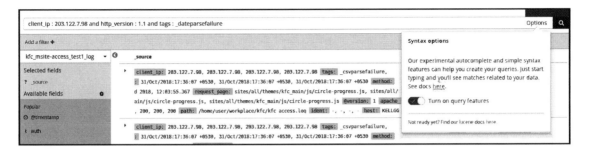

In the preceding image, we can enable the syntax options by clicking on the options link in the search textbox. Once it's enabled, we can construct our queries in the search textbox. See the following expression:

```
client_ip : 203.122.7.xx
```

In the preceding expression, I am matching all the documents where `client_ip` matches the given value. This is very handy when we want to search a particular IP address or a specific field value from the complete dataset. In the same way, we can pick any field and match it with any value to find all those documents where the field has the same value. Now, let's see how we can combine more than one query using `and` or `or`:

```
client_ip : 203.122.7.98 and http_version : 1.1 and tags :
_dateparsefailure
```

In the preceding expression, I added three different field matches and combined them with `and` so that we should get only those records where all of these criteria are matched. Instead of `and`, we can also use `or` if we want results that match any of the matching criteria. The matching results on the documents are highlighted in yellow to make it easy to identify them.

# Filter Your Data

You can filter your data using the `add a filter` link, which is under the search textbox. Using this option, we can apply the filter on the data on any field, in the data, and we can also give the filter a name to make it more meaningful while displaying the filtered data.

The following screenshot shows the filter box, using which we can create a filter and apply it:

Perform the following steps to apply a filter on your dataset:

1. Click on the **add a filter** link under the search textbox. This will open a filter box.
2. Under the fields dropdown, select the field name on which you want to apply the filter. After selecting the field name, the operators dropdown will appear.
3. From the operators dropdown, select the required option, such as **is, is not, exists**, or **does not exist**.
4. From the values dropdown, select the value on which you want to filter the data.
5. Provide any label to the filter. You can provide any meaningful name to this filter.
6. Click on the **Save** button to apply the filter.

The filter screen also gives us the option to convert this filter into an Elasticsearch query DSL so that we can directly modify the query and write complex expressions directly from that filter screen. To convert the filter option to a query, click on the **Edit Query DSL** link in the filter box. After clicking on **Edit Query DSL**, we can see the following:

In the preceding screenshot, you can see the Elasticsearch query expression that's created from the graphical filter applied on the data. We can modify this query directly or replace it with any other value. Under the label, we have a delete icon, using which we can delete the current filter.

We can apply as many filters as we want to drill down into our data; it provides us with the toolset to dissect our data to explore anything. Also, the filter labels are handy as we can give each filter a relevant name, using which we can later understand the impact of a filter without seeing the actual implementation of it filter.

# Save Your Filtered Data

When we explore the data, we can apply multiple filters and use the search box query to drill down into the desired result set from the data. Now, imagine we don't have the option to save this result set along with the search criteria; what will happen every time we need to do all those activities to extract the desired result set from the complete data? Luckily, we have the save functionality in Kibana, which helps us to save different datasets along with the applied filters, queries, and time-based filters.

# Save Your Search

Saving searches helps us to save us time as we can open the saved data and can see the result as per the pre-configured filters, queries, and time-based filters.

Now, let's see how we can save search results and open them again to analyze the data. Once we're done with the search and want to save the current set of data with all applied filters, we need to click on the **Save** button in the top-right corner, which will open the following screen:

The preceding screen shows the save search screen. Here, we have the option to provide the name of the search in form and click on the **Save** button to save it. Here, I have added the search name as **destination_ip_and_port** and saved it. Once the search data is saved, you can see the search name in the top-left corner. See the following screenshot:

In the preceding screenshot, you can see the name of the search data, **destination_ip_and_port**. You can check it to ensure that your result is saved successfully. Now that this result is saved, you can open it at any time. To open search data, click on the **Discover** link in the left menu and then click on the **Open** link in the top-right menu option. This will open the following screen:

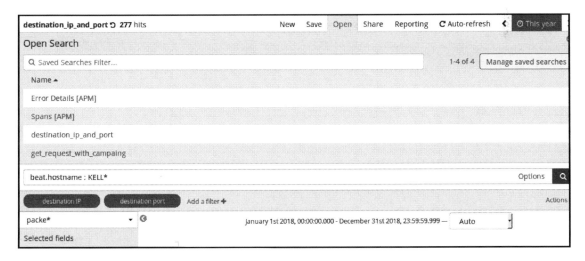

In the preceding screenshot, we can see a list of save searched data, where we can click on any name we want to open. Here, the name is required to describe what's happening in this saved search, so we need to provide a meaningful name every time we save the search data.

# Manage Saved Searches

We can manage our saved searches by clicking on the **Manage saved searches** link on the open search screen. This will open the **Saved object** screen; the following screenshot shows the saved object:

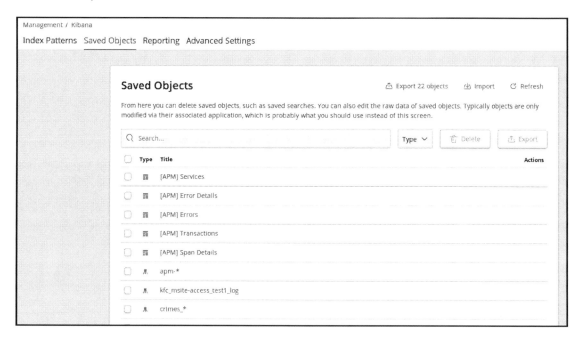

The preceding screenshot shows the **Saved Objects** screen, where we can see all the saved searches and preconfigured visualizations. We have different links to perform different operations, such as an export link with the number of objects to export these saved searches and preconfigured visualization data. After that, we have the import link, using which we can import any exported search object. When we click on the export option, it shows us the option to export different components, such as visualization, dashboard, search, and index-pattern, along with the count for each of them. We can select or unselect them before exporting the saved object. The following screenshot shows the saved object's export option:

In the preceding screenshot, we have the option to choose separate components, such as visualization, dashboard, search, and index-pattern. After choosing the required components to export, we can click on the **Export All** button. This will download the export.json file. We can use this file to import these components back into Kibana.

# Summary

In this chapter, we covered Kibana Discover and how we can explore data using **Discover**. We discussed how to discover your data using the different options provided in Kibana Discover, such as how to limit the number of fields to display in order to focus on the dataset, which is more relevant than the other fields. Then, we saw how to expand a document display to check all available fields, along with the option to view the surrounding documents and a single document. From this screen, we can apply a filter on any field. Then, we covered different ways to dissect the data, such as filtering the data by applying the time-based filter, filtering the data based on different document fields, and applying a query on your dataset. We explored how to save the search data so that the search data and filter options are available for reuse. After saving the search data, we can export it from Kibana and save it into a file that can later be imported back into Kibana.

In the next chapter, we'll look at how to create different types of visualizations. We'll learn about different types of visualizations, such as basic charts, data, maps, and time series. We'll also cover how to create these visualizations using a dataset imported in Kibana. Once we've created some charts, we'll explore how we can edit, delete, share, or embed a chart on any page.

# 4
# Visualizing Data

In earlier chapters, we covered how to install different components of the Elastic Stack, and then configured Beats and Logstash to push data into Elasticsearch. After pushing the data into Elasticsearch, we covered Kibana Discover to explore data by applying query and filter on the data, and after that saved the search data for further use. So, basically, we have set the stage by creating the index pattern to create Elasticsearch index data availability in Kibana. Now, we are going to discuss the most important features of Kibana, using which we can create meaningful visualizations with the data.

There are different types of visualizations we can create using Kibana, such as basic charts under which we can create an area, heat map, horizontal bar, line, pie, vertical bar, and so on. Then under data category of visualization, we have data table, gauge, goal, and metric types of visualization. After that, we have maps, where we can create a coordinate map, region map, and so on. Under time series, we have Timelion and Visual Builder and at last, we have visualization options, such as controls, markdown, tag cloud, and vega, which comes under the other category in Kibana. We will try to udnerstand the most common visualizations. So, let's start with the Kibana visualization, where we will cover all commonly used visualizations and will start with basic charts. We will cover the following topics in this chapter:

- **Data Aggregation**: Here, we will cover how Kibana uses Elasticsearch aggregations to create different visualizations.
- **Visualization Types**: They provide us with different options for visualizations, which are as follows:
    - Area Chart
    - Heat Map
    - Pie Chart
    - Data Charts
    - Data Table
    - Metric
    - Tag Cloud

- **Inspect Visualizations**: Using `inspect`, we can see the actual values behind the visualizations
- **Share Visualization**: Using the `share` option, we can share the visualization and can embed it in any web page
- **Dashboard**: We can club different visualizations to create a dashboard

# Data visualization

In the previous chapter, we covered Kibana Discover, using which we can explore our data to understand it better. Using Discover, we can do lots of things, but when it comes to showing your complete data in a single view, we need a visualization. So, when we talk about data visualization, we mean a process to display data in the form of graphical charts, bars, maps, or any sort of visual representation. Data visualization provides us a way to understand more about the data, such as what is the trend, anomalies in data, or the pattern of the data quite easily.

# Data aggregation

Now, if we talk about Kibana Visualize, it uses Elasticsearch aggregation for creating visualizations. So, basically, in the background, we are applying Elasticsearch aggregations using the Kibana UI interface. In Kibana, we use two types of aggregations: metric and bucket. **Bucket aggregation** groups documents in different buckets using conditions such as range, terms, filters, and so on; **Metric aggregation** calculates a value based on the applied aggregation method, such as count, sum, average, and so on. Under bucket aggregation, we have sub-buckets, which can be a **split series** or **split chart**. A split series is to splits a global dataset into different small datasets. In the case of a pie chart, we call it **split slices**, as it creates multiple slices in a pie chart. Then, we have a split chart, using which we can create multiple charts on the same $x$ or $y$ axis. We can separate the charts in the form of rows or columns for showing multiple charts.

# Visualization types

Before creating any visualization, we should know what we are trying to achieve from the visualization. Such as, if we want to see the percentage of 400 status codes the visitors to our site are getting, or want to know which different browsers are being used to access the sites. Then, we need to decide the type of visualization we should use for our use case, because the same data can be represented in different visualization types, but we should pick the best-suited one, using which we can have a clear idea about the data.

We have different types of charts, such as an area chart, where we can specify the area utilization; a heat map, which is again a graphical representation where individual values are represented as colors; a horizontal bar chart represents the data in the form of horizontal bars; a line chart draws the graph in the form of lines; a pie chart can be used to represent part of a whole; and, last, we have a vertical bar chart, which represents data in the form of vertical bars. A tag cloud is a display of word clouds for a particular field. You can select the visualization type as shown in the following screenshot:

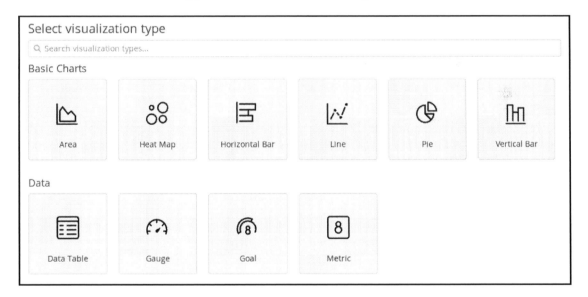

The preceding screenshot shows the visualization type page, from where we can select the type of visualization we want to create. Now let's understand the different types of visualization and how we can create visualizations using each of them.

## Area chart

To create the an area chart, you need to do the following:

1. Click on the **Visualize** link from the left menu of Kibana. This will open the page with the listing of visualizations if you have any.
2. Click on the plus button to create a new visualization.
3. Click on the **Area** box under **basic charts** on the **Select Visualization type** page. This will open the index selection page.
4. Now, we can either select index or do a new search for creating the visualization or we can pick any saved search for creating the visualization. For now, we can click on a new index such as filebeat.
5. This will open the new visualization screen, where we need to configure the settings as per our requirements.
6. Under the $y$ axis, select count under aggregation and change the custom label to **Total requests**.
7. Now, under the $x$ axis, select **Terms** under **Aggregation** and select **apache2.access.response_code** under **Field** options.
8. Provide the size for the chart as per your requirements, as this may vary.
9. Under custom label, provide a relevant label, such as **Response code.**
10. Now, click on the **Apply Changes** button to apply these changes and create the Area Chart visualization. This will open the following screen:

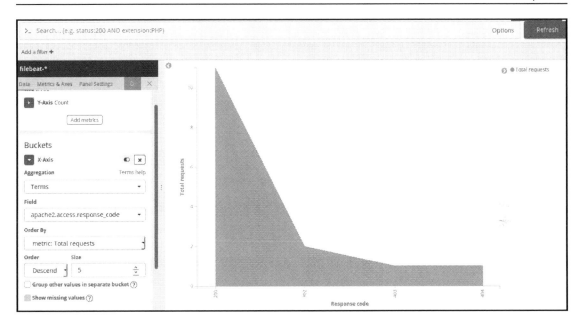

In the preceding screen, we can see the $x$ axis is response code, whereas the $y$ axis is the total number of requests:

1. Once the visualization is created, we can and should save it for the future. To save the visualization, we need to click on the **Save** button on the top menu's options.
2. This will open the saved popup, where we can add the name and click on the save button to save the visualization.
3. Once this visualization is saved, we can later open it or can use it for dashboard creation. This way, we can create an `Area Chart` under **Visualization**.

In the same way, we can create a line chart or bar chart, as they represent the same type of plot. We can click on the **Metrics & Axes** link to open the **Metrics** page, from where we can change the chart type to area, bar, or line chart. The following screenshot shows the page with the **Chart type change** option:

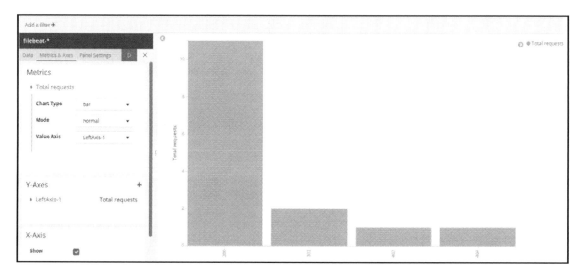

In the preceding screenshot, we can see that, we can change the chart type to an area, a bar, or a line chart. Currently, it is set to a bar chart, and this is the same area chart that we have seen in the previous section. Now we will cover how to create a heat map visualization in Kibana.

# Heat map

Heat map is a kind of data visualization where we use colors to represent different sets of data values. These visualizations are quite easy to understand as color is used to differentiate the differences in data values. In Kibana, we can easily create a Heatmap, and to create one, we need to do following:

1. On the **Select Visualization Type** page, under **Basic Charts**, click on the **Heat Map** option. This will open the index selection page.
2. Select the filebeat index, as we want to see the number of requests against the Apache response codes.

3. This will open the new **Heat Map** visualization screen.
4. Under the *y* axis, select **Count under aggregation** and change the custom label to **Total requests**.
5. On the *x* axis, under **Buckets**, select **Terms** under aggregation and select **apache2.access.response_code** under **Field** options.
6. Provide the size as per your requirements, as this may vary.
7. Under **Custom** label, provide a relevant label, such as **Response code.**
8. Now, click on the **Apply Changes** button to apply these changes and create the **Heat Map** chart visualization. This will open the following screen:

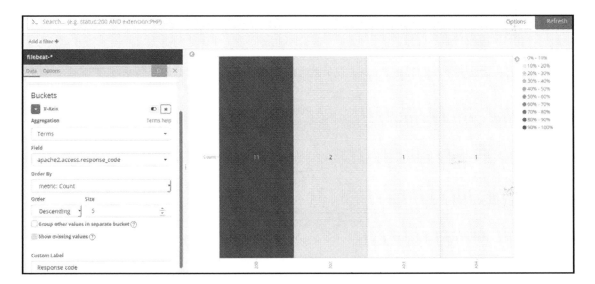

From the preceding screenshot, we can see in red that we have 11 requests for the 200 response code, and then different colors for different response codes from Apache. In this way, we can create a Heat map for any set of data fields, as per our requirements.

# Pie chart

A pie chart is important when we want to show the percentage of something. If we take our earlier example, where we wanted to plot in 100% response how much percentage of response code 200, 302, 403, and 404. So, if we plot this as a pie chart, we get something such as the following screenshot:

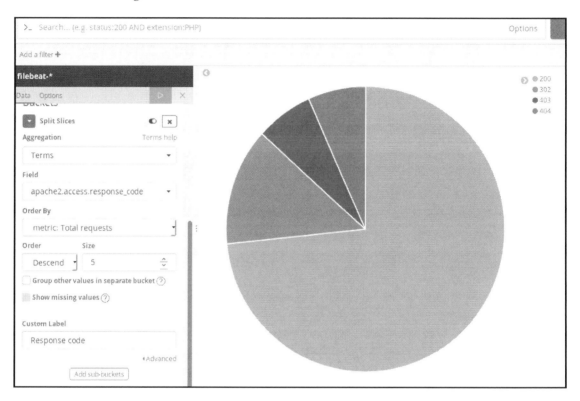

The preceding screenshot shows the pie chart representation of the same dataset we used for the area chart and the heat map chart. If we want to create this pie chart, then we need to do the following:

1. Select the **Pie** option from select visualization type page. This will open the index selection page.
2. Select the filebeat index, as we want to see the number of requests against Apache response codes.

3. This will open the new **pie chart** visualization screen.

4. Under the *y* axis, select **Count under aggregation** and change the custom label to **Total requests**.

5. Click on **Split Slices** under buckets, choose **Terms under aggregation**, and select **apache2.access.response_code** under field options.

6. Set order by and provide the size as per your requirements, as this may vary.

7. Under **Custom** label, provide a relevant label, such as **Response code**.

8. Now, click on the **Apply Changes** button to apply these changes and create the pie chart visualization, as shown in the preceding screenshot.

9. We can change the pie chart into a donut chart by clicking on the options link and then selecting the donut option. It will convert the pie chart into a donut chart as shown in the following screenshot:

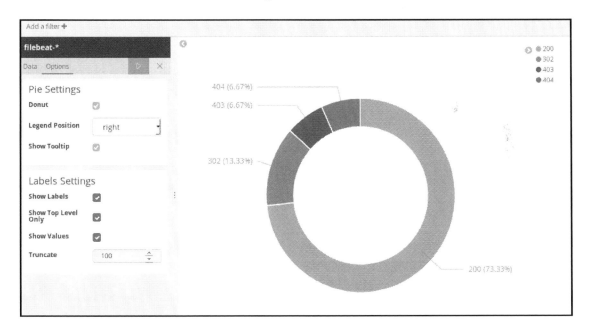

The preceding screenshot shows the donut chart, which was converted from a pie chart; also, we have enabled the tooltip by clicking on the **Show Tooltip** option under the options link. This way, we can create a pie or donut chart under Kibana Visualize. We can add sub-buckets to create multi-stack pie charts.

# Data table

A data table is again a nice way to represent data in a tabular form. The graphical chart helps us to take quick decisions, while the data table is there to check the actual figures. When we want to create a dashboard for any specific use case, we should include the charts, as well as data tables referring to the same data points, in the dashboard. On the dashboard, by using charts, we can get the insight, and by clicking on specific regions, we can drill down into the region-specific details, and our data table helps us to see the actual data that created the chart.

In Kibana, we need to do the following to create a data table:

1. Under the **Data** section on the **Select visualization type** page, click on the **Data Table** option. This will open the index selection page.
2. Select the filebeat index, as we want to create a data table using filebeat apache2 log data. This will open the new **New visualization** screen.
3. Under **Metrics**, select count option against aggregation and change the custom label to **Total requests**.
4. Click on **Add metrics** if we want to add one more metrics. If required, you can add more metrics in your data table.
5. Click on the **Split Rows** link under **Buckets** to add columns.
6. Choose terms under aggregation and select **apache2.access.response_code** or any field you want to display under the **Field** options.
7. You can add more columns in the same way.
8. Now, click on the **Apply Changes** button to apply these changes and create the **Data Table** type visualization, as shown in the following screenshot:

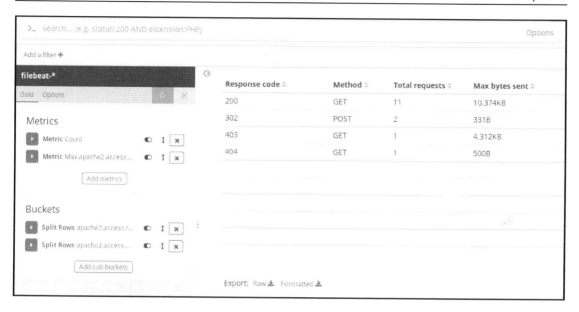

The preceding screenshot shows the data table display of Apache log data, where we can see the response code, method, total requests, and max bytes sent. We can export this data table in the form of an unformatted or formatted CSV file by clicking on the respective option below the table display. We can change the ordering of data by clicking on the up or down arrow next to the field name in the data table. After creating the data table as per our requirements, we can save it, to use later.

# Metric

The metric visualization type, under data is to basically display a count or numbers against any field. We can show any count, sum, the average, or a different possible set of values for a field. Let's take an example where we want to show the count of GET and POST requests in Apache. In this scenario, we can easily use the metric type of visualization and to add this, we need to do the following:

1. Click on the **Metric** option under the **Data** section on the **Select visualization type** page. This will open the index selection page.
2. Select the filebeat index as we want to create a data table using filebeat apache2 log data. This will open the **New visualization** screen.

3. Under **Metrics**, select **Count** option against **Aggregation** and change the **Custom Label** to `requests`.

4. Click on **Add metrics** if we want to add one more metric. If required, you can add more metrics to your data table.

5. Click on the **Split Group** link under **Buckets** to add columns.

6. Choose **Terms** under **Aggregation** and select **apache2.access.method** or any field you want to display.

7. Now, click on the **Apply Changes** button to apply these changes, which will create the **Metric** type visualization, as shown in the following screenshot:

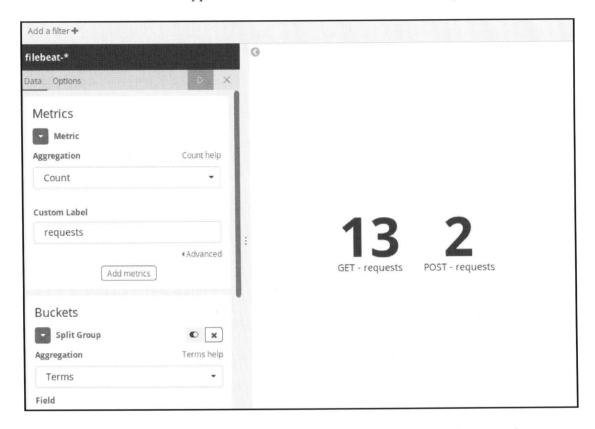

The preceding screenshot shows the metric data display, which shows the get and post requests. Using this visualization, we can easily get an idea about the types of requests we are getting. This way we can show any numerics display using Kibana metric type data visualization.

# Tag cloud

Tag Cloud is also a very good and intuitive visualization option. We can configure it to show keywords, which can be clicked and filtered using the Tag Cloud visualization. We need to do the following for creating a Tag Cloud:

1. On the select visualization type screen, click on the **Tag Cloud** option under **Other Categories**. This will open the index selection page.
2. Select the filebeat index as we will pick the keywords from this index again. This will open the **New visualization** screen.
3. Select **Count** for **Aggregation** under the **Metrics** option and provide the label as **Response Codes**.
4. Click on the **Tags** link under buckets.
5. Choose terms under aggregation and select **apache2.access.response_code** or any field you want to display.
6. Change the custom label to **Apache** or anything else, as per your requirements.
7. Now, click on the **Apply Changes** button to apply these changes, which will create the **Metric** type visualization, as shown in the following screenshot.
8. Click on the **Save** button in the top-right corner to save the visualization:

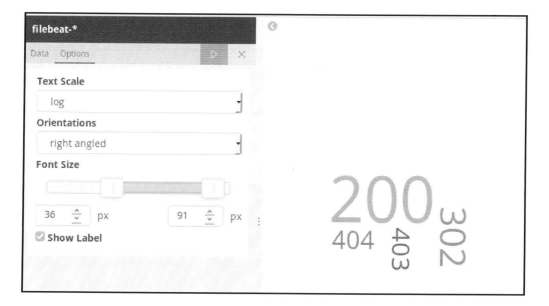

From the preceding screenshot, we can see the response codes, such as 200, 302, 403, and 404, are visible, but code 200 is quite prominent; this is because the 200 request count is higher than any other request code. We can change the default font settings and orientation by clicking on the **Options** link and changing this parameter as per our requirements. Like we can change the lower and higher font values or text orientation to single, right-angled or multiple, we can also change the text scale.

# Inspecting visualizations

We can inspect a visualization to see the actual data behind the graphical visualization. We can also see the statistics, such as the number of total hits, index pattern, query time, request time, and so on, or the actual request JSON of Elasticsearch and the actual response JSON of Elasticsearch. We can also download the formatted or raw CSV data from the **inspect** screen. The following screenshot shows us the data view of **Inspect**:

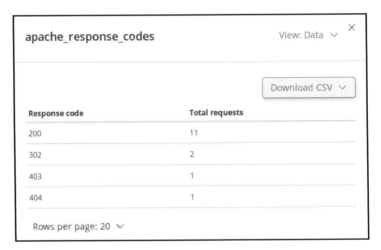

The preceding screenshot shows the inspect view of the data for the **apache_response_codes** area chart we created earlier. In this view, we can see the tabular data display's response code and total requests. From this data view screen, we can download the raw or pre-formatted CSV data. We can change this data view to the requests view by changing it through the **View** dropdown in the top-right corner of the page. After changing it to requests mode, we can see the statistics, request, and response options.

The following screenshot shows us the default request view:

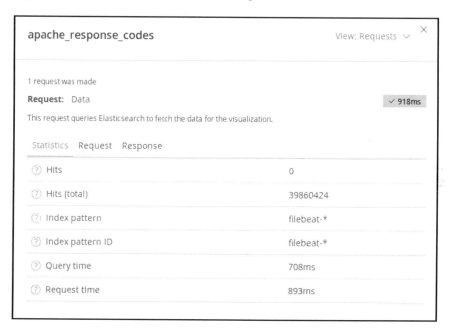

In the preceding screenshot, we can see request statistics data such as total hits, index pattern, index pattern ID, query time, request time, and so on. After that, we have the request option where we can see the actual JSON request of Elasticsearch, and, finally we have a response option, which shows the Elasticsearch response JSON.

# Sharing a visualization

Once the visualization is created, we can embed it on any web page using the share option of the visualization. To share a visualization, we need to click on the share button on the top-right corner of the page. This opens the **share this visualization** popup with two options: **Embed code** and **Permalinks**. The Embed code option is present, using which we can copy the iframe code to integrate it into any web page. There are two different options under embed code: the first is **Snapshot**, using which we can save the current state of the visualization, and no change on current visualization after we create the snapshot. Another option is **Saved Object**, which shows the most recent saved version of the visualization, and if we do an update in the visualization it will be reflected in the shared version. We have a short URL option, using which we can create a short URL of the embedded code.

Let's say we want to embed the most recent link of
the **apache_response_code** visualization, which shows the area chart with response codes
on the *x* axis and total requests on the *y* axis. So, now we need to click on the share button
and select the **Saved object** option, and then we can click on **Short URL** to check this option
for creating short URLs. After making all these changes, we can click on the **Copy IFrame
code** button, which will copy the following iframe embed code for the visualization:

```
<iframe
src="http://localhost:5601/goto/b2f6a08b8fd523d0310887de09ac1f12?embed=true
" height="600" width="800"></iframe>
```

We can copy the preceding code and can use it on any web page to display the
visualization on the custom page. Now, as we have the iframe code lets create a web page
as `kibana.html` by writing very simple code as follows:

```
<html>
<head>
<title>This is a demo visualization page.</title>
</head>
<body>
    <h2>Kibana Visualization display</h2>
    <h3>This is my custom web page</h3>
    <iframe
src="http://localhost:5601/goto/b2f6a08b8fd523d0310887de09ac1f12?embed=true
" height="600" width="800"></iframe>
</body>
```

In the preceding code, we are creating a simple web page with a title and a heading, and
after the heading, we are including the iframe code to embed the Kibana visualization in
this web page. After saving the HTML file, open it in a browser to display the web page; it
will show something like the following screenshot:

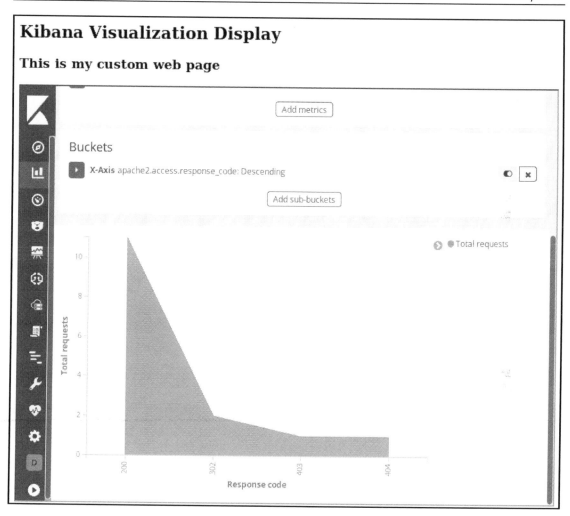

In the preceding screenshot, we are showing a simple web page with the area chart visualization that we created in Kibana. This way, we can embed as many visualizations as we want in a web page. In the same way, we can copy the snapshot iframe code and then it can also be embedded in a web page.

Another option under share is **Permalink**, which provides us the link for the current visualization. There are two options to create the permalink; the first is **Snapshot**, which creates the snapshot of the current state of the visualization, so if any changes happen after creating the permalink, those will not be available to the snapshot permalink. The second is **Saved Object**, where the permalink will show most recent saved version of the visualization, so, after sharing the permalink, if the visualization is updated, then it will be reflected in the permalink created using the **Saved object** option.

# Dashboard

Up to now, we have covered how to create different types of visualizations in Kibana; now, let's see how we can integrate different types of visualizations to create a dashboard. Dashboards are quite useful as they provide us a single view to monitor the KPI. To create a dashboard in Kibana, we need to do following:

1. Click on the dashboard link from the left menu, which will open the dashboards page with a list of existing dashboards.
2. We can click on any existing dashboard to open the dashboard. But as we want to create a new one, click on the **Create a new dashboard** button in the top-right corner of the page.
3. This will open a blank page with the message **This dashboard is empty. Let's fill it up!**.
4. Click on the **Add** button to add the visualizations. This will open the following screen of **Add Panels**:

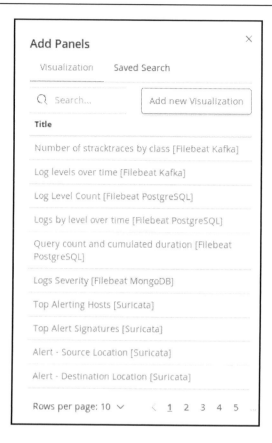

In the preceding screen, we have the visualization and saved search options, from where we can add already save visualizations or a new visualization.

- We can search the visualization using the search box and can click on the name of the visualization to add it to the dashboard panel.

- In this way, we can add all those visualizations we want to show on the dashboard panel. The following screen shows the dashboard view after adding five visualizations to the dashboard panel:

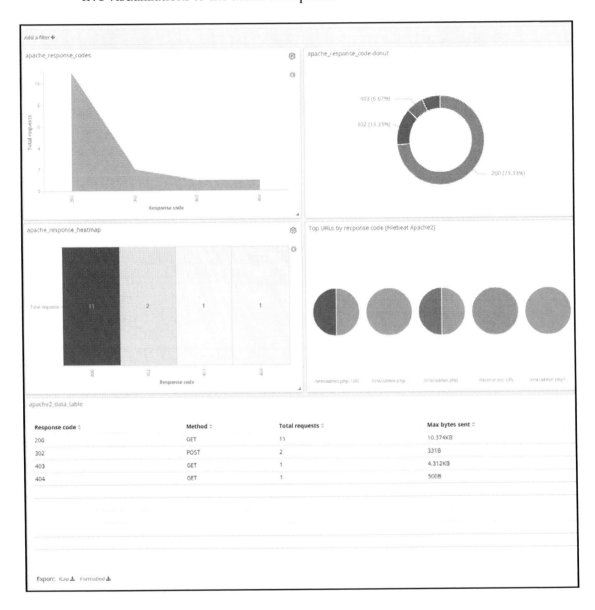

In the preceding screenshot, we have an area chart, pie chart, heat map, and data table, which are on the dashboard for monitoring HTTP responses through the Apache log file.

1. Once the dashboard is created, we can save it by clicking on the save link under the top-right.

2. We can click on the edit link to edit the dashboard. In edit mode, we can do the following things:

   - Rearrange the visualization panels by dragging and dropping them to the desired location
   - Edit the visualization by clicking on the edit visualization link under the panel settings
   - We can inspect individual visualization data by clicking on the inspect link under the panel settings
   - The visualization can be viewed in full screen by clicking on the full screen link under the panel settings
   - We can change the label of the visualization by clicking on the customize panel link under the panel settings
   - We can also delete any visualization from a dashboard by clicking on the delete from dashboard link under the panel settings

3. We can apply the dark theme,**hide/unhide** panel titles, or **show/hide** margins between panels by clicking on the **Options** link under top-right links.

4. Using the share option, we can share the dashboard in the same way as we did for the visualization. The following screenshot shows the embedded dashboard on a web page:

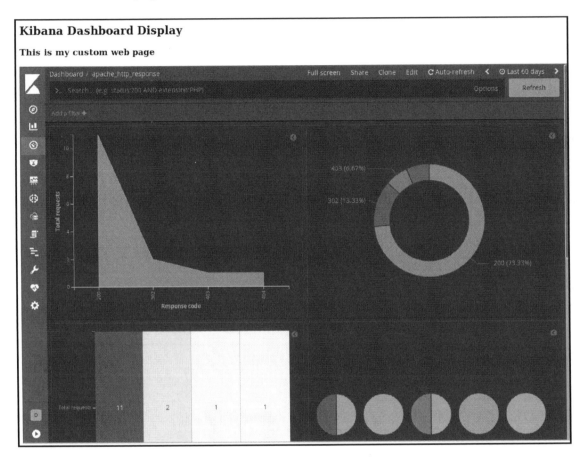

The preceding screenshot shows the Kibana dashboard, which is embedded inside a custom web page; using the embed link, we can embed a dashboard or individual visualizations in any web page, as per our requirements.

# Summary

In this chapter, we covered how to visualize the data once it is available in Kibana, after creating the index pattern. We started with basic charts, where we covered creating chart such as the area chart, heat map, and pie charts, and so on. We also covered how we can transform one type of chart into another by giving examples of an area chart, line chart, and bar chart; in the same way, we can change a pie chart into a donut, or vice versa. After that, we have covered data tables, using which we can generate a tabular visualization of data, to which we can add additional metrics columns, along with actual data columns. Then, we covered the metric type of visualization, where we can display some metric value, and tag cloud, which can be used to display a word cloud with a link to filter the data.

We covered dashboard creation by integrating visualizations and arranging them in the desired order. We also covered the panel settings option under, each panel on the dashboard. Panel's such as inspect, edit visualizations, customize panel, delete from the dashboard, and so on. We have seen different options such as the dark theme, margins between panels, and hide/unhide panel titles under **Options** link. Then, we also covered how the complete dashboard can be embedded in a web page.

In the next chapter, we will cover X-Pack installation and its features. We will see what machine learning is and how we can use it to detect anomalies in data and spot future trends.

# X-Pack with Machine Learning

# 5

In this chapter, we will cover the features of X-Pack, as Elastic Stack comes without X-Pack. We will discuss some of the features that are missing if we are not using X-Pack's security, which can be activated by the multi-tenant element, by enabling the user and roles, and we can also control what needs to be displayed for each role. After security, we have monitoring, which helps us to oversee our Elastic Stack and provides an audit to check whether everything is working correctly. We can supervise the Elasticsearch overview, nodes, indices, and Kibana overview, instances, and so on. From this overview page, we can obtain the details by clicking on the links on nodes, indices, overview, instances, and so on.

Reporting is another feature that is available under X-Pack. Reporting can be used to generate PDF reports from visualizations and dashboards, both of which can be downloaded from the reporting section under the management link on the left menu. After reporting, we have machine learning, which is a vital feature as it allows us to identify anomalies in the data while also generating future trends. machine learning is a category of algorithms that work on a set of data to create a mathematical model, which can be used to predict future trends. It also provides watchers, which help us to produce alerts and to check certain thresholds in any field data.

So, here we will cover the following topics:

- **Introduction to X-Pack:** In the introduction, we will introduce X-Pack and discuss why it is required.
- **Installation:** Here, we will see the installation process of X-Pack.
- **Security:** Under security, we will learn how to secure our Elastic Stack using X-Pack:
    - **Role management:** Here, we can create different roles for different access rights
    - **User management:** This is what we will use to create different users and assign them the required roles

- **Monitoring:** Using monitoring, we can monitor our Elastic Stack and obtain details such as the indexing rate.
- **Alerting:** Using alerting, we can create different types of alerts based on certain conditions.
- **Reporting:** Reporting enables us to generate CSV and PDF reports from our visualizations and dashboards.
- **Machine learning:** Using machine learning jobs, we can discover anomalies in our data and predict future trends:
  - **Single metric job:** These machine Learning jobs are created using a single field of the index
  - **Multimetric job:** In multimetric jobs, we can use more than one field for creating the machine Learning job

# Introduction to X-Pack

X-Pack extensions can be installed on top of the Elastic Stack to enable security, monitoring, reporting, alerting and graphs, and more. X-Pack is introduced from Elastic Stack version 5.0.0. Before that, we have separate plugins such as Shield, Marvel, and Watcher that can be installed as per the requirements. In X-Pack, all these features are bundled together. Another issue before X-Pack came was having to match the versions of each plugin, but now all we need to do is install the right version of X-Pack and all features will be available without any version issues. The first step to explore X-Pack is to install it on your Elastic Stack. So, let's first install X-Pack and then we can start exploring.

# Installation

We need to install X-Pack for Elastic Stack 6.2 or older versions because, from version 6.3 onward, X-Pack comes as a default distribution with Elastic Stack. So, in Elastic Stack 6.3 and onward, we get all the free features enabled by default, while other features can be enabled by installing X-Pack. We can also opt for a 30-day trial period of X-Pack, which will still allow us to run all the features of X-Pack. To install X-Pack with Elastic Stack if our Elastic Stack version is 6.2 or older, we need to do the following:

1. We have to install X-Pack on both Elasticsearch and Kibana, so begin by installing X-Pack on Elasticsearch.

2. Next, move to the Elasticsearch installation directory and execute the following command:

```
bin/elasticsearch-plugin install x-pack
```

This expression will install the X-Pack plugin with Elastic Stack.

3. After installing X-Pack, start the Elasticsearch service.
4. Generate default passwords by running the following command:

```
bin/x-pack/setup-passwords auto
```

After running the preceding command, please make a note of the Elasticsearch and Kibana user passwords.

5. Now, as we have installed X-Pack on Elasticsearch successfully, let's install it on Kibana by executing the following command:

```
bin/kibana-plugin install x-pack
```

6. After installing X-Pack on Kibana, we need to add `elasticsearch.username` and `elasticsearch.password` under the `kibana.yml` file.
7. After updating the `kibana.yml` file, start Kibana.
8. After installing and configuring X-Pack, when we open the Kibana interface, it shows us the following login interface:

Here, we have the screen that must be used to log in using the Elastic username and password. This login screen will come after successful installation of X-Pack because the default Elastic Stack has no login interface, and the Kibana interface opens automatically without any login screen. In this way, X-Pack provides us with the security to restrict access through users and roles.

# Security

Security is a fundamental feature of X-Pack as, without it, anyone can open any URL. Security will give them unlimited access, including to index patterns, data, visualizations, and dashboards of Kibana. During X-Pack installation and setup, we need to create the default user credentials, but after that, we have dedicated user and role options from which we can create roles and users, and then can assign these roles to the users. To create users and roles, we need to click on the management link from the left menu, which opens the following **Management** screen:

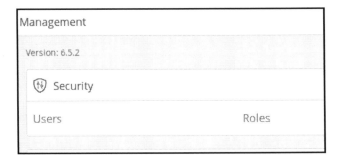

Here, we can see the **Management** screen, where we have users and roles option under **Security**. From this screen, we can manage users as well as roles. So, now let's see how we can manage users and roles.

# Role management

We can initiate the role management process by clicking on the **Roles** link under **Security** on the **Management** screen. The following screen shows the **Roles** page:

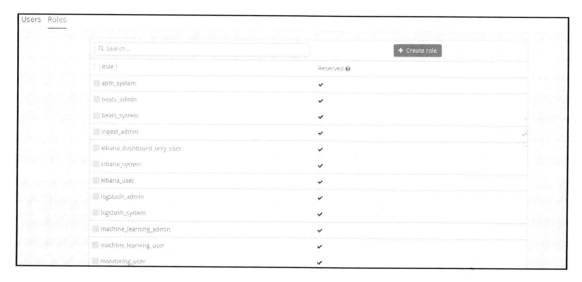

Here, we can see that the screen displays a list of all the available roles, with a **create role** button to create a new role. To create a new role, we need to do following:

1. Click on the **Create role** button, which will open the create role screen.
2. Enter the **Role name** that you wish to create.
3. Under the **Elasticsearch** section, select **Cluster privileges** from the dropdown.
4. Set the **Run As privileges** option if you want to work on behalf of other users.
5. Under **Index**, set the privileges you want to grant access to this role.
6. Under **Kibana**, set the minimum privileges for all spaces.
7. Then click on the **Create role** button to create the role.
8. This will create the role and will open the roles listing page.
9. We can click on the newly created role to open it in edit mode. The following screen shows the role screen:

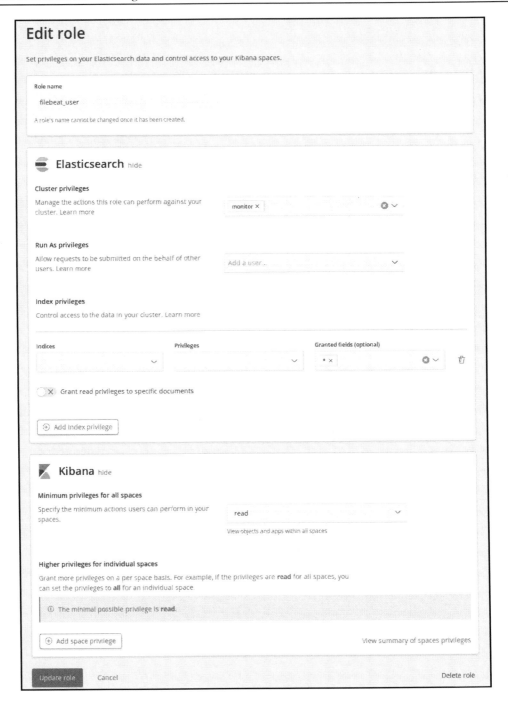

Here, we can see the **Edit role** screen, where we can update the role. This is where we can create the roles as per our requirements. For instance, if we wanted to give access to only a specific index, then a new role can be created here to put that in place. We can also limit set access restrictions to the index. For instance, we can provide read-only access so that only users with certain roles can view or edit an index. Once the role is created, we can assign it to users so that we can restrict them.

# User management

User management is also an essential feature of X-Pack as it provides us with the security to access the Kibana and Elasticsearch cluster. To create users, we need to click on the **Users** link under **Security** on the **Management** page. This will open the user listing page, as shown in the following screenshot:

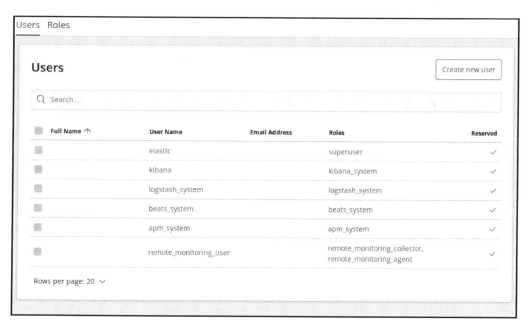

Here, we can see the default user list that was created during X-Pack setup. These are default users that we cannot edit or delete. To create a new user, we need to do the following:

1. To create a new user, click on the **Create new user** button.
2. Fill the new user form with the **Username, Password**, **Full name**, and **Email Address**.

3. Select the desired roles from the roles in the dropdown. We can select multiple roles here.
4. Click on the **Create User** button to create the new user.
5. A new user will be created, and then the user listing page will open.
6. From this listing, we can select the newly-created user and can delete it by clicking the **Delete** button above the listing.
7. We can click on the user to open the user screen in edit mode.
8. We can delete the user from the edit screen by clicking on the **Delete user** link. The following screenshot shows the edit user screen:

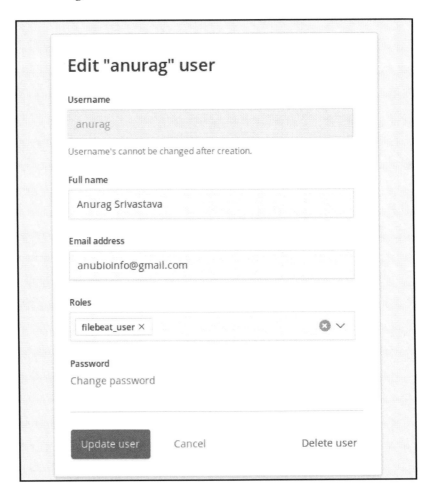

Here, we can see the edit user screen, where we can update user details, change the user password, or delete the user. We can also update user roles from this edit screen by adding new roles or by removing existing roles.

# Monitoring

Monitoring is another essential feature of X-Pack, although some key monitoring is available for free with Elastic Stack, X-Pack provides all the monitoring capabilities available. Monitoring allows us to understand how our Elastic Stack is running and where we need to improve. To view Elastic Stack monitoring, we need to click on the **Monitoring** link from the left menu, which opens the following screen:

Here, we can see brief details of Elasticsearch and Kibana, where we have the overview, nodes, and indices sections for Elasticsearch, and the overview and instances for Kibana. This is just the basic information for these sections, and if we want more detail for each of them, then we need to click on the title of the section and click on the **Overview** link.

The following screenshot shows detailed information from the Elasticsearch overview:

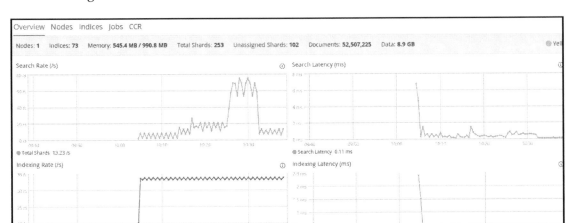

Here, we can see the details of the Elasticsearch overview, which shows the graphs for search rate, search latency, indexing rate, indexing latency, and more. This information is vital, and it helps us to tweak the Elasticsearch performance. In the same way, we can see the details for the nodes and indices of Elasticsearch. Monitoring details of Kibana can also be viewed by clicking on the **Overview** or **Instances** link under **Kibana**. Using these details, we can improve the performance as we know the area that needs enhancing, and monitoring helps us to understand how our Elastic Stack is performing.

# Alerting

For alerting, we have watchers that notify us when given conditions are met. The condition can be anything, such as if a field value crosses a certain threshold or if there is an anomaly in the data. In any such condition, we want a notification so that appropriate action can be taken. With the Kibana UI, we can set a watch for any condition, but in the background, we can have a periodic Elasticsearch query that monitors the data and checks whether the given condition is met and acts upon the result. An action could be to send an email, notify a third-party tool such as Slack, or log entry.

Watcher history is maintained in the Elasticsearch index, where we can get the complete information of a watcher, such as when it was executed, the results of its execution, whether the given condition was met, and what the output of the watcher was. When we install X-Pack, a watcher is enabled by default. Now let's see how a watcher can be created in Kibana. So, we need to do the following three things to configure a watch:

1. Schedule a watch on single or multiple fields.
2. Set a condition to match.
3. Configure the action to be performed.

So, when creating any watch, we need to do these three things. In the first step, we need to select the index and fields to which we want to apply the watch. Then, we have to set the condition to be checked in a periodic manner and follow this up with the action that would be performed when the given condition is met. In Kibana, we can create a watch using the following steps:

1. Click on the **Management** link from the left menu.
2. From the **Management** page, click on the **Watcher** link under the Elasticsearch section.
3. On the **Watches** page, click on the **Create threshold alert** button.
4. This will open the **Create a new threshold alert** page. Add the name, select the indices, and set the **time** field.
5. Set the schedule by setting the duration. By default, it is set at 1 minute, but we can change this to any value.
6. Under the **Matching the following condition** section, set the condition that needs checking using the interactive interface.
7. Now set the action to be performed by selecting the action from the **Add new action** dropdown. We can send email, log a message, or send a message to Slack using this option.

Now take a practical example where we want an alert if CPU time spent on a process goes above 70%; for this metric, we need to refer to Metricbeat data. So, on the watch creation page, put the label as `cpu_usage_more_than_70_percent` or any other label that is meaningful. Then, select `metricbeat` **under** `indices to query` and pick the timestamp field as `@timestamp`. Next, select the duration as, for example, 10 seconds. Refer to the following screenshot for these settings:

### Create a new threshold alert

Send an alert when a specific condition is met. This will run every 10 seconds.

**Name**

cpu_usage_more_than_70_percent

| **Indices to query** | **Time field** | **Run watch every** |
| --- | --- | --- |
| metricbeat-6.5.2-2018.12.30 ✕ | @timestamp ▾ | 10 ⇕ seconds ▾ |

Use * to broaden your search query

Here, we can see how to configure the watch name and its data source, along with the duration to run the watch for.

After setting the data source, it's time to create the condition on which this watch will perform a specific action. As we are creating the watch to track the percentage of CPU time spent by a process to check whether it goes above 70%, we need to add the condition on `system.process.cpu.total.pct`. To set this condition, we need to set the `max()` function for **WHEN** to check, with a max value of `system.process.cpu.total.pct`, by setting this field under **OF**. Then, select all documents for **OVER** and set `0.7` for **IS ABOVE** to check whether the max value of the field goes beyond `0.7`. Finally, set `1 minute`, or any duration, for **FOR THE LAST** duration. The following screenshot shows the matching condition criteria:

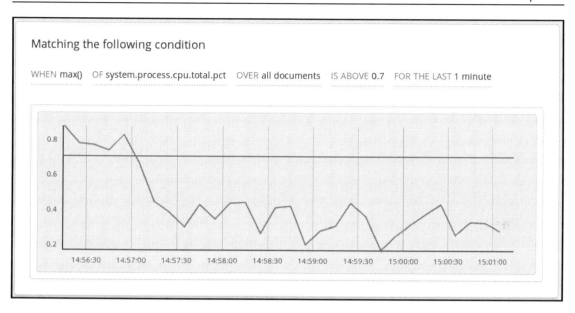

Here, we can see how to set the matching condition as well as a graph visualizing the condition. The red line indicates the condition, and the blue bar shows the `system.process.cpu.total.pct` values over a 10-second interval. Whenever this blue bar touches or crosses the red line, the condition will be met and the action will be performed. Now let's see how we can configure the action based on this condition.

As we have set the condition to match, let's next create the action to be performed. We can send an email to any email address, log a message to the log file, or send a message over Slack. So, let's use the configure email action. Before setting it up, we need to add the SMTP credential in the `elasticsearch.yml` file. I have configured the Gmail SMTP accounts and added the following configuration in my `elasticsearch.yml` file:

```
xpack.notification.email.account:
    gmail_account:
        profile: gmail
        smtp:
            auth: true
            starttls.enable: true
            host: smtp.gmail.com
            port: 587
            user: b******@gmail.com
            password: b*****@****
```

After that, click on **E-mail** option from the add new action dropdown. Add the email address under the **To e-mail address** text box. Edit the **Subject** section as per the requirements and add the message in the body section. After adding these details, click on the **Test fire an e-mail now** button to test the email flow. Afterward, click on the **Save** button to save the watch. The following screenshot shows the action section of the watch:

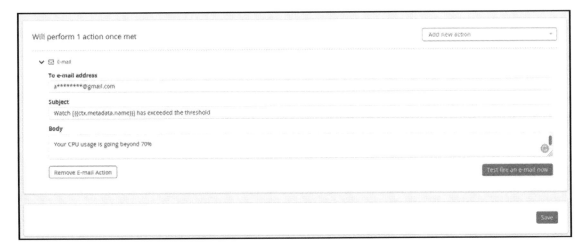

Here, we can see how to set up the email, and the watch will send the email to a given address once the condition is met.

# Reporting

X-Pack reporting is useful as we can get CSV or PDF reports for Discover data or Dashboard views using the reporting option. There are different ways to download CSV or PDF reports:

- Under the Discover tab, once we have saved the data, the CSV report can be downloaded by clicking the **Share** link from the top-right menu, then clicking on the **CSV Reports** link, and then clicking the **Generate CSV** button. This will generate the CSV report for the saved Discover data.

- From the Visualize screen, after saving the visualization, we can generate the PDF report by clicking on the **Share** link from the top-right menu, clicking the **PDF Reports** link, and then clicking the **Generate PDF** button.
- We can also download the PDF report from the Dashboard screen. To do so, we need to click on the **Share** link from the top-right menu, then click the **PDF Reports** link, and then click on **Generate PDF**.

Once the report is created, we can download it by clicking on the **Management** link from the left menu. Next, click on the **Reporting** link under the Kibana section, which will open the following screen:

| Objects  Spaces  Reporting  Advanced Settings | | | |
|---|---|---|---|
| **Reports** | | | |
| **Report** | **Created at** | **Status** | **Actions** |
| apache_http_response dashboard | 2018-12-30 @ 05:04 PM elastic | completed at 2018-12-30 @ 05:04 PM | 🖫 |
| apache_response_code-donut visualization | 2018-12-30 @ 05:03 PM elastic | completed at 2018-12-30 @ 05:03 PM | 🖫 |
| ML Apache2 Access Data search | 2018-12-30 @ 04:59 PM elastic | completed at 2018-12-30 @ 04:59 PM | 🖫 |
| ML Apache2 Access Data search | 2018-12-30 @ 04:56 PM elastic | completed at 2018-12-30 @ 04:56 PM | 🖫 |
| apache_http_response dashboard | 2018-12-22 @ 11:35 PM elastic | completed at 2018-12-22 @ 11:35 PM | 🖫 |

Here, we can see all the reports that have been generated from the Discover, visualize, or dashboard screens. We can download these reports from here by clicking on the **Download** link under the **Actions** column. In this way, through reporting, we can generate these reports and can send them to anyone.

# Machine learning

Elastic Stack uses a proprietary machine learning algorithm, which we can utilize for finding any anomaly, statistical rarity, or unusual behavior in data. This feature is activated once we install X-Pack with our Elastic Stack. Machine learning works with time series-based data by reading the normal trend in the data to create the baseline. Once the baseline is created, it can predict the future trend and detect anomalies. This way, we can anticipate behavior for different reasons; for instance, we may be running a website and want to how many users will be registered to our website in two years, or how much traffic is expected in the coming weekend. In this way, machine learning can provide us with vital information just by reading our data. Now let's see how we can create the machine learning jobs using our Elasticsearch data. We need to do the following to create a new machine Learning job:

1. First of all, we need to click the **Machine learning** link from the left menu, which will open the **Job Management** page of machine learning.
2. On this page, we can see a listing of the already-created jobs, if we have already created any.
3. To create a new job, we need to click on the **Create new job** button.
4. This opens the data selection page, where we can pick from the index or the saved search. We can select any index pattern from here. This will open the following screen:

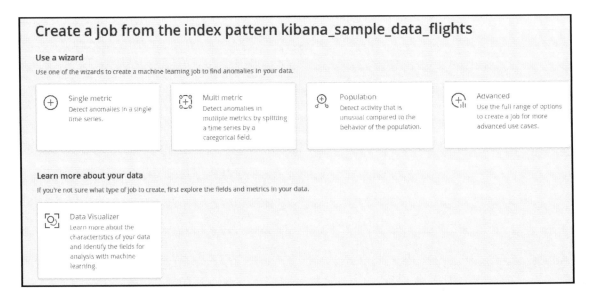

Here, we can see the different options for creating a new machine learning job:

- We can create different types of jobs, such as single-metric, multimetric, population, or advanced.
- If we are not sure about the data and fields to which we should apply machine learning, then we can use the data visualizer to help us understand our data before creating the Machine Learning job.

Now let's see how we can create single-metric and multimetric jobs.

# Single-metric job

Single-metric jobs are those where we use a single field to run the machine learning job. Take the example of **Kibana sample data flights**. This data comes with Elastic Stack, which can easily be downloaded. So, from the wizard screen, click on the single-metric box and set the **Aggregation** as **Max**, the **Field** as **FlightDelayMin,** and the Bucket span as **15m**. This will show the chart with the field metric displayed. Next, add the job name and description. The following screen shows the job creation page:

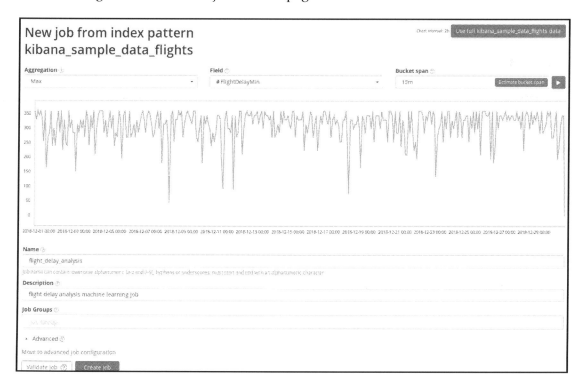

After filling the details, click on the **Create job** button. This will create the job, and we can see the outcome by clicking on the **View results** button. The following screenshot shows the result of the single-metric Machine Learning job:

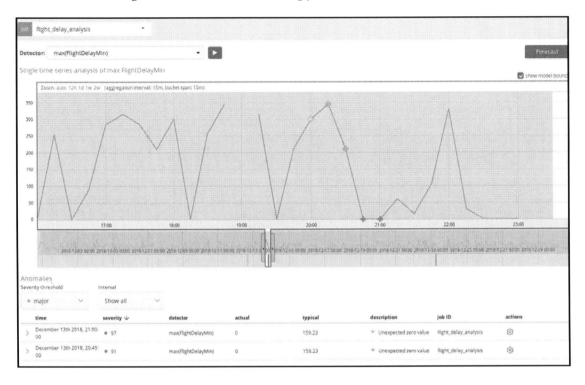

Here, we can see the trend of data with anomalies as markers, and following the graph, we can see the details of the anomalies. Above the graph, we have a forecast button, which creates the future trend for the data. The following screenshot shows the data forecast:

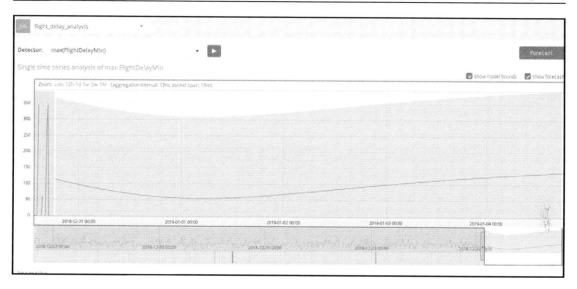

Here, we can see the future trend for the data based on the analysis. In this way, we can analyze any data and can see future trends by checking the forecasting graph.

# Multimetric job

A multimetric job is a Machine Learning job where we can analyze multiple data points at the same time. If we want to examine the average ticket price and flight duration, for example, we need to work with the **AvgTicketPrice** and **FlightTimeMin** fields, and we can use both of them for a multimetric job. So, to create a multimetric job, we need to click on the multimetric box from the job selection wizard, then click on the fields we want to add. Select the field to split the data by. I have picked **Carrier** to split the data points for different carriers. Select the bucket span to provide the name and description of the job.

The following screenshot shows the multimetric job creation page:

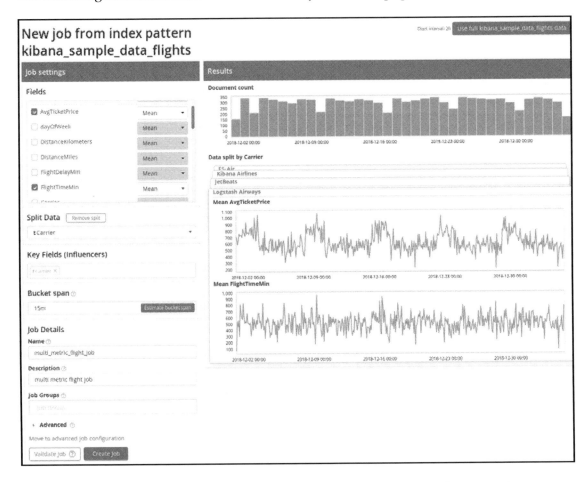

Here, we can see that average ticket price and flight time graphs are split as per the different carriers. Now click the **Create job** button to create the multimetric job, which will open the success screen with a **View results** button. Click on that to open the anomaly explorer page. Here, anomalies are shown as colored boxes; you can click on any colored box to see the details in the form the graphs and a table showing anomaly data. The following screenshot shows a page with anomalies in the **FlightTimeMin** and **AvgTicketPrice** data points:

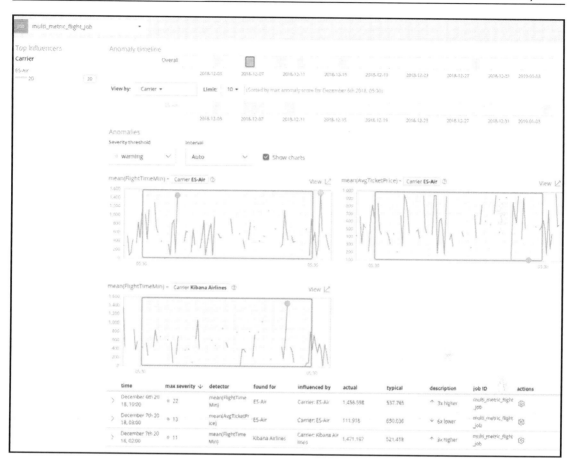

Here, we can see the blue and yellow dots on the graph, for which details can be seen upon mouse hover. Below the graph, we have a tabular representation of the anomalies with details such as typical value and actual value. This way, we can analyze our data through single-metric or multimetric Machine Learning jobs.

In the same way, we can create a population job where a trend is created as per the population, and then the unusual behaviors are compared against it. The job creation and result is quite similar to a multimetric job. Advanced jobs allow us to use all options to customize the job; it should be noted that this is only necessary in certain use cases.

# Summary

In this chapter, we have covered how X-Pack adds additional features to an existing Elastic Stack setup. We started with the introduction of X-Pack, and after that, we covered the installation process of X-Pack. Then we covered the different features of X-Pack, such as security. Under security, we covered user and role management by creating users and roles, and then we assigned roles to the users. After security, we covered monitoring in detail. Then we covered alerting, configuring a watch to send alerts via email. After alerting, we covered reporting and the generation of CSV or PDF reports. Finally, we covered Machine learning, where we created single-metric and multimetric jobs and analyzed data by finding the anomalies and predicting future trends. In Chapter 6, *Monitoring Applications with APM*, we will cover monitoring applications with APM.

# 6
# Monitoring Applications with APM

**Application Performance Monitoring (APM)** is there to monitor application performance and is built on top of the Elastic Stack. APM is used to monitor application and software services in real time. We just need to configure the APM agent for the application, and after that the agent will collect and send various application-related information, such as HTTP requests, database queries, and the response time for the requests, to the APM server. Although many of the details we can get using browser developer tools, in Elastic APM we have many additional advantages: it also collects unhandled errors and exceptions, which is very important for application stability, and also the search option provides us an edge in pinpointing any issues. In this chapter, we will cover an introduction to and implementation of APM using a Django project.

APM, along with Logstash and Beats, provides us with full-stack monitoring where we can cover everything from applications, databases, servers, and different logs. It provides us with end-to-end information, which can be configured on a single dashboard, and we can set alerts on important indicators. This way, we can save time and resources by configuring APM to monitor our application, along with other system and process-related monitoring, which ultimately increases productivity because we can have a single platform to monitor everything. Let's start by configuring APM with the Django framework in Python.

In this chapter, we are going to cover the following:

- **APM Agents**: We will cover how APM Agents can be configured with an application and how they send data to APM Server
- **APM Server**: We will cover an introduction to, and use of, APM Server:
    - **Install APM Server**: We will cover the steps to install APM Server
    - **Run APM Server**: Here, we will cover how to run APM Server
    - **Configure dashboard using APM Server**: In this section, we will cover how to configure predefined dashboards in APM
    - **APM Server monitoring**: Here, we will cover how to start monitoring the APM server
- **Elasticsearch**: We will cover how Elasticsearch works for an APM setup
- **Kibana**: Here, we will see how Kibana contributes to an APM setup
- **Configure Django application with APM**: Here, we will take an example with the Python Django framework to explain how you can configure APM

# APM components

APM mainly consists of four different components, which work together to monitor the application. These components are as follows:

- APM Agents
- APM Server
- Elasticsearch
- Kibana

We can configure APM Agents as a library for an application, to send application metrics and data to the APM Server, from where data can be pushed to the Elasticsearch Cluster. Once data is pushed to Elasticsearch, we can view and analyze the data using the Kibana APM UI or Dashboard. Now, let's understand what each of these components does and how they can be configured with a different application:

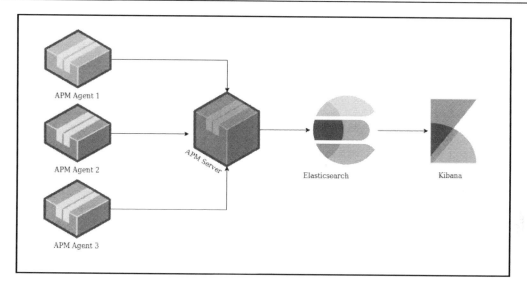

In the preceding diagram, we have three APM Agents, which are sending data to a central APM Server, from where data is pushed to an Elasticsearch cluster, and then using Kibana, we can visualize and analyze this data through the APM UI or the Dashboard of Kibana.

# APM agents

APM agents are open source libraries that can be configured in the application, as they are built in same native language; so, for Python Django, we have an APM agent that is written in Python. We can install them as a library in the application in the same way we install other libraries. Once they are configured, they collect data and errors from the application at runtime. APM Agents can buffer data for a period of time and send it to the APM Server. APM Server then sends the data to the Elasticsearch cluster, from where Kibana fetches the data and shows the metrics through a dedicated APM UI or through the Dashboard, which we can configure in Kibana.

The Elastic company has applied a dedicated team to developing APM Agents, and it is growing to cover more and more languages and frameworks, but for now it supports some frameworks and languages, such as Django and the flask frameworks of Python, Rails, Rack, RUM - JS, Java, Go, Node.js, and Go. Once we install them as a library in the framework, such as in Django, the agent collects real-time data and errors and sends them to APM Server. We can open the APM setup instructions by clicking on the **Setup Instructions** button on the APM page of Kibana. It opens the instructions to set up APM Server and APM Agents.

The following screenshot shows the setup of APM Agent for the Django framework in Python:

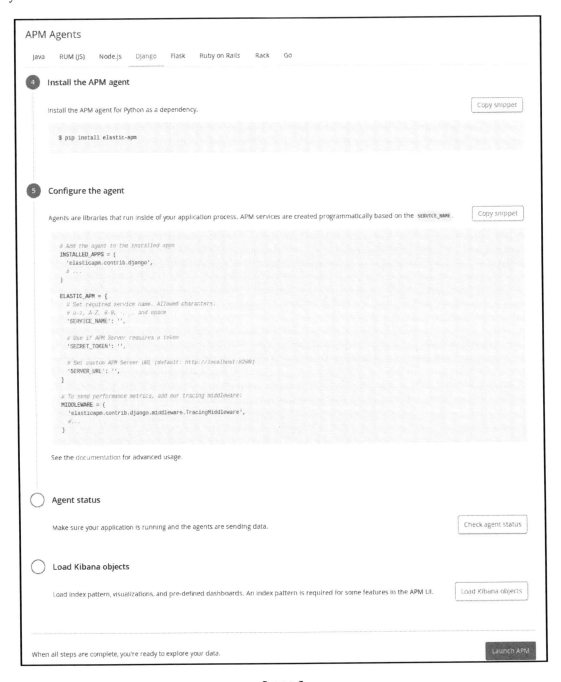

APM Agents

Java    RUM (JS)    Node.js    Django    Flask    Ruby on Rails    Rack    Go

**4** Install the APM agent

Install the APM agent for Python as a dependency.                                        Copy snippet

```
$ pip install elastic-apm
```

**5** Configure the agent

Agents are libraries that run inside of your application process. APM services are created programmatically based on the SERVICE_NAME.    Copy snippet

```
# Add the agent to the installed apps
INSTALLED_APPS = (
    'elasticapm.contrib.django',
    # ...
)

ELASTIC_APM = {
    # Set required service name. Allowed characters:
    # a-z, A-Z, 0-9, -, _, and space
    'SERVICE_NAME': '',

    # Use if APM Server requires a token
    'SECRET_TOKEN': '',

    # Set custom APM Server URL (default: http://localhost:8200)
    'SERVER_URL': '',
}

# To send performance metrics, add our tracing middleware:
MIDDLEWARE = (
    'elasticapm.contrib.django.middleware.TracingMiddleware',
    #...
)
```

See the documentation for advanced usage.

○ **Agent status**

Make sure your application is running and the agents are sending data.                    Check agent status

○ **Load Kibana objects**

Load index pattern, visualizations, and pre-defined dashboards. An index pattern is required for some features in the APM UI.    Load Kibana objects

When all steps are complete, you're ready to explore your data.                          Launch APM

The preceding screen shows the steps to install APM Agent, configure it, check the status, and load Kibana objects. Using this page, we can easily set up APM for our environment, as this setup page is very straightforward, Using it, we can set up and test the APM configuration.

# APM Server

APM server is written in Go and is freely available with Elastic Stack. APM agent sends data to the APM Server in the form of JSON through the HTTP API. APM server listens on port 8200, which is the default port. Once APM Server receives the data from different APM Agents, it clubs them, using the data, to create documents and push them to Elasticsearch. To build APM Server, Elastic has used the Beats framework; the APM Server also utilizes Beats functionalities.

APM server is a separate component that sits between APM agents and Elasticsearch, unlike Beats, which can directly interact with Elasticsearch. There are many reasons why APM server is important, as it can easily be scaled because typically they are configured on the dedicated machine. It also prevents browsers from interacting with Elasticsearch directly, to avoid any security risks and control the amount of data before sending it to Elasticsearch. APM Server also helps us to buffer the data whenever Elasticsearch goes down. As we have different types of agents, which work in different languages, it is quite important to make it compatible and then send to it Elasticsearch. The APM setup instructions page can be opened by clicking on the **Setup Instructions** button on the APM page at the Kibana APM link. This page shows the instructions to configure APM Server and APM Agents for application monitoring.

The following screen shows the APM Server setup instructions:

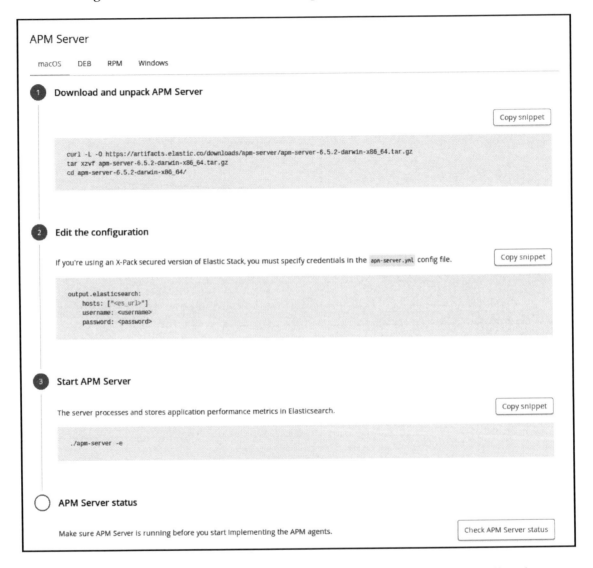

This screen shows the instructions page, from where we can find steps to install and configure APM Server on different platforms. It has four steps, in which it explains how to download and unpack APM Server. It also explains how to edit the APM Server configuration, then the command by means of which we can start the APM Server, and then the option to check the status of the APM Server.

# Install APM Server

To install the APM Server, we have to first download the APM Server from the download section of Elastic (`https://www.elastic.co/downloads/apm`). After downloading the APM Server, we need to extract the downloaded package. APM Server can also be installed using repositories for YUM or APT, and we can also install it on Windows as a service.

## APT

We can install APM Server through the APT repository using the following steps:

1. In the first step, the public signing key needs to be downloaded, and then we need to install it:

   ```
   wget -qO - https://artifacts.elastic.co/GPG-KEY-elasticsearch |
   sudo apt-key add -
   ```

2. Then, we can install the `apt-transport-https` package on Debian:

   ```
   sudo apt-get install apt-transport-https
   ```

3. After that, the repository definition has to be saved under `/etc/apt/source.list.d/elastic-6.x.list`:

   ```
   echo "deb https://artifacts.elastic.co/packages/6.x/apt stable
   main" | sudo tee -a /etc/apt/sources.list.d/elastic-6.x.list
   ```

4. Install APM Server after updating the repository by executing the following command:

   ```
   sudo apt-get update && sudo apt-get install apm-server
   ```

5. To autostart APM Server after every reboot, run the following command:

   ```
   sudo update-rc.d apm-server defaults 95 10
   ```

This way, we can install the APM Server using the APT repository.

## YUM

We need to do the following to install APM Server using the YUM repository:

1. Download the public signing key using the following command:

```
sudo rpm --import https://packages.elastic.co/GPG-KEY-elasticsearch
```

2. Then, under the `/etc/yum.repos.d/` directory, we need to create a `.repo` extension and then add the following expression:

```
[elastic-6.x]
name=Elastic repository for 6.x packages
baseurl=https://artifacts.elastic.co/packages/6.x/yum
gpgcheck=1
gpgkey=https://artifacts.elastic.co/GPG-KEY-elasticsearch
enabled=1
autorefresh=1
type=rpm-md
```

3. We can now install the APM Server using the following command:

```
sudo yum install apm-server
```

4. To configure it on auto start after every reboot, we need to run the following command:

```
sudo chkconfig --add apm-server
```

In this way, APM Server can be installed using the YUM repository.

## Install APM Server on Windows

APM Server can be installed on Windows with the following steps:

1. First, we need to download the APM Server from the download section of Elastic (`https://www.elastic.co/downloads/apm`).
2. Extract this downloaded zip under `C:\Program Files`.
3. Rename the long directory name, with the version name appended to it, to a clean name such as `apm-server`.

4. Open PowerShell with admin rights and run the following command:

```
cd 'C:\Program Files\apm-server'
.\install-service-apm-server.ps1
```

This way, we can install APM Server on a Windows machine.

# Run APM Server

To run APM Server, we need to run the following command:

```
./apm-server -e
```

We can start the APM Server after executing the preceding command. Once APM Server is started, then it will connect to Elasticsearch on localhost port 9200. For listening the APM agent through API, it exposes the port 8200. But again, this is the default setting, which we can change by executing the following command:

```
./apm-server -e -output.elasticsearch.hosts=ElasticsearchAddress:9200 -E
apm-server.host=localhost:8200
```

We can also change this configuration by modifying the apm-server.yml configuration file. We can modify the APM Server port, or Elasticsearch host and port, by modifying the following section of the file:

```
apm-server:
  host: localhost:8200

output:
  elasticsearch:
    hosts: ElasticsearchAddress:9200
```

So once the apm-server.yml file is modified, we need to restart the APM service.

# Configure dashboard using APM Server

Pre-configured dashboards can be loaded using APM Server, and for that we need to configure the Kibana endpoint. This dashboard configuration can also be done through the apm-server.yml config file using the following setting:

```
setup.dashboards.enabled: true
```

We can also load the dashboard by running the following setup command from the system:

- **deb and rpm:**

```
apm-server setup --dashboards
```

- **mac:**

```
./apm-server setup --dashboards
```

- **docker:**

```
docker run docker.elastic.co/apm/apm-server:6.5.4 setup --
dashboards
```

- **win:** Change directory to the location where you installed APM Server, and run the following command:

```
PS > .\apm-server.exe setup --dashboards
```

This way, we can load the Dashboard for APM.

# APM Server monitoring

Using the X-Pack Monitoring feature, we can set up the APM Server for monitoring. We have already covered monitoring in Chapter 5, *X-Pack with Machine Learning*. To set up APM Server monitoring, we need to do the following:

1. We can send the monitoring data to Elasticsearch by creating a user with the apm_system role. The same thing can be done using the inbuilt apm_system user.

2. We need to add xpack.monitoring settings to the APM Server configuration file. We need to enable the Elasticsearch output settings in case it is not enabled. Using the following settings, we can enable APM Server monitoring:

```
xpack.monitoring.enabled: true
```

3. Open Kibana and click on the **Monitoring** link in the left menu. Verify the monitoring metrics by clicking on the APM Server link. This way, monitoring can be configured for APM Server.

# Elasticsearch

APM Server sends metric and error data received from the APM agents to the Elasticsearch Cluster. We can utilize the search and aggregation capabilities of Elasticsearch to analyze APM data. So basically, Elasticsearch stores all the APM data, which can then be analyzed or visualized in Kibana.

# Kibana

For APM data, we have two options in Kibana to visualize it: first using a dedicated APM UI, which is available under the APM link in the left menu, or the default Dashboard, which is mainly used to visualize other data sources. As we have covered how to install and configure APM with Elastic Stack, now we will cover how to configure a Python Django application with APM.

# Configure Django application with APM

I will take an example of an application for blog creation and listing API using Python Django framework. First, we have to install the APM agent for Python Django:

```
pip install elastic-apm
```

Then, we have to configure the agent with the Django application; we need to make the following changes in the settings.py file:

```python
# Add the agent to the installed apps
INSTALLED_APPS = (
   'elasticapm.contrib.django',
   # ...
)

ELASTIC_APM = {
   # Set required service name. Allowed characters:
   # a-z, A-Z, 0-9, -, _, and space
   'SERVICE_NAME': 'django application',

   # Use if APM Server requires a token
   'SECRET_TOKEN': 'mysecrettoken',

   # Set custom APM Server URL (default: http://localhost:8200)
   'SERVER_URL': 'http://localhost:8200',
}
```

```
# To send performance metrics, add our tracing middleware:
MIDDLEWARE = (
    'elasticapm.contrib.django.middleware.TracingMiddleware',
    #...
)
```

Using these changes in the `settings.py` file, we can configure the APM agent with the Python Django application. For creating the blogs, I am using the following request with the `POST` method:

```
{
    "title": "This is my test Blog.",
    "content": "I am creating this blog to test the Elastic APM",
    "author": 1
}
```

After executing this request, my Django application gives me the following response:

```
{
    "status_code": 200,
    "message": "SUCCESS",
    "blog": {
        "id": 15,
        "title": "This is my test Blog.",
        "content": "I am creating this blog to test the Elastic APM",
        "author": 1,
        "create_date": "2019-01-06T17:24:40.108092Z",
        "update_date": "2019-01-06T17:24:40.108129Z"
    }
}
```

This response comes when we post the blog creation request to the Django web API. Now, when we open the APM screen in Kibana, it shows the following screen:

In the previous screen, we can see the service name of the application, which we have given to the APM agent configuration in the `settings.py` file of the Django application. We can see the details by clicking on the service named **django application**, which opens the following screen:

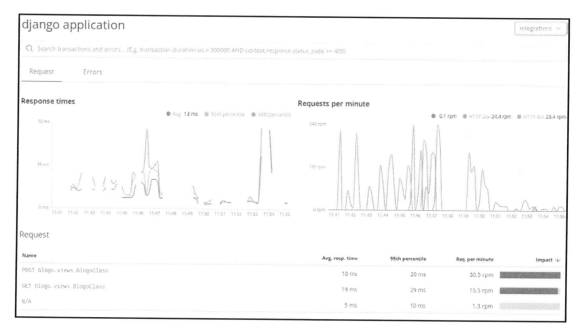

In the preceding screen, we can see the graphs that display **Response times** and **Requests per minute** and below the graph, it shows different GET and POST requests, along with unknown requests. We can click on any of the request links to open the details page for that particular type of request. The following screen shows the details of POST requests:

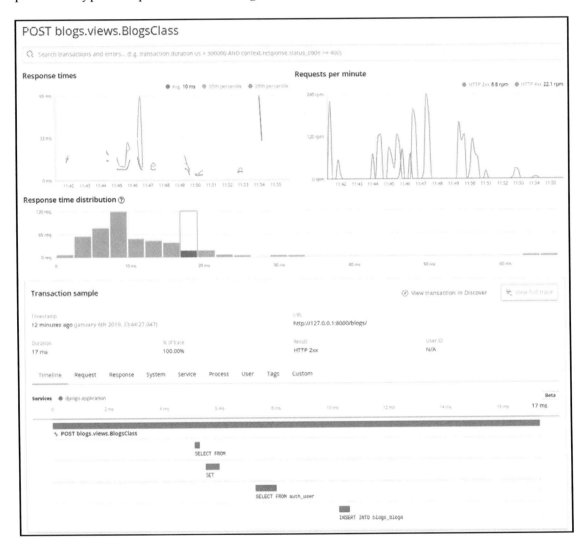

In the preceding screen, we can see the details of the POST request APIs. It shows the response times, requests per minute, response time distribution, and transaction sample with different views such as timeline, request, response, system, service, process, user, tags, and custom. In the same way, we can click on the GET request link to see the details of GET requests. We can also apply search filters on our dataset using the search box on top of the page; see the following screen:

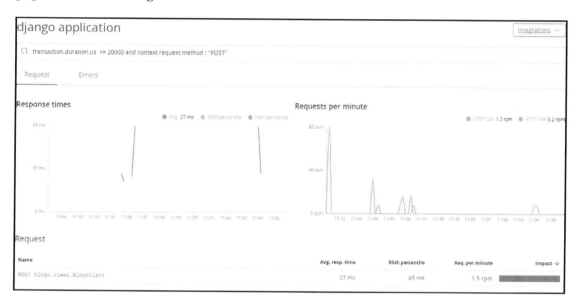

In the previous screen, we have applied the filter on transaction duration and request method to see the filtered result. We can also open the Kibana Dashboard view of APM, like the APM transactions dashboard which is quite similar to the APM UI screen view. From the APM Dashboard view, we can click on the **view spans** link to see the span details; see the following screen:

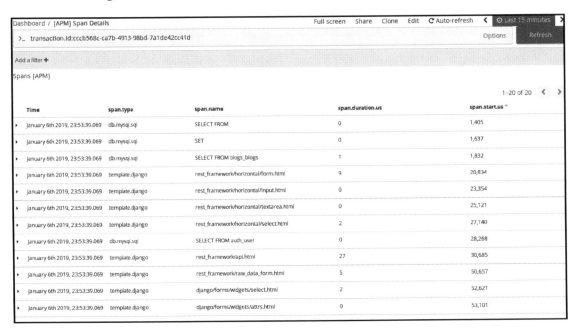

In the previous screen, we can see the span detail of GET requests. They are organized in the form of a tabular view with **Time**, **span.type**, **span.name**, **span.duration.us**, and **span.start.us** fields. We can expand the view to see the details for a particular span.

# Summary

In this chapter, we covered Elastic APM and explained how we can monitor an application. We started with the APM components, which are APM Agents, APM Servers, Elasticsearch, and Kibana. After that, we covered each of them in detail. APM Agents are open source libraries that can be configured in any of the supported languages/libraries. Currently, we have support for Django and flask frameworks of Python, Java, Go, Node.js, Rails, Rack, RUM - JS, and Go. We can configure them to send application metrics and errors to APM Server. Then, we covered APM Server, which is again open source software, written in Go.

The main task of the APM Server is to receive data from different APM Agents and send it to the Elasticsearch Cluster. Elasticsearch takes the APM data, which can then be viewed, searched, or analyzed in Elasticsearch. Once data is pushed to Elasticsearch, we can display it in Kibana using the dedicated APM UI or through the Kibana Dashboard.

In `Chapter 7`, *Kibana Advanced Tools*, we will cover various tools that are available in Kibana, such as Timelion, by means of which we can play around with time-series data, and DevTools, by means of which we can execute Elasticsearch queries from the Kibana console. Also, we will see how the Grok debugger can be used to write Logstash log matching patterns.

# Kibana Advanced Tools

**7**

In this chapter, we will cover other important features of Kibana, including Timelion and Dev Tools. We will cover how to use Timelion for time-series data and create different graphs by chaining different functions. Timelion provides us with flexibility, by means of which we can club data from different indices together to plot them on a graph. Using Timelion, we can get some interesting answers to questions that are difficult to answer—such as the difference between the data this Sunday and last Sunday—using default visualizations of Kibana. We can also compare the current data with older data, such as four-hour old data or one-week old data. We can plot on the basis of the moving average over a certain duration; it provides us with a smooth graph if the data plot is not easy to understand. Using Timelion trends, we can plot the trend of data by applying regression on the time-series data.

Dev tools is there to write and execute Elasticsearch expressions directly from the Kibana interface. It provides type hinting, which makes it quite easy to query Elasticsearch data. Dev Tools also provides us with auto-indent and the option to copy the expression as cURL, which we can paste into the terminal to execute directly. It has an input section for writing Elasticsearch expressions and an output section where the results of those expressions are displayed. In this chapter, we will see how Dev Tools can be used to increase productivity and how, using Timelion, we can create complex visualizations on time-series data by chaining some of the methods available for Timelion.

In this chapter, we are going to cover the following topics:

- Timelion
- Use cases of Timelion
- Dev Tools

# Timelion

Timelion is a data visualizer designed to work on time-series data. Timelion works on different independent data sources and can be used to integrate them in a single visualization. In Timelion, we have a relatively simple expression language that helps us to retrieve time-series data, perform mathematical calculations, and change the color, label, and other calculations in order to create complex visualizations that are difficult to create using Kibana visualization. We have a Help link in the top-right corner; we can open the function reference by clicking on the link. The following screenshot shows the function reference:

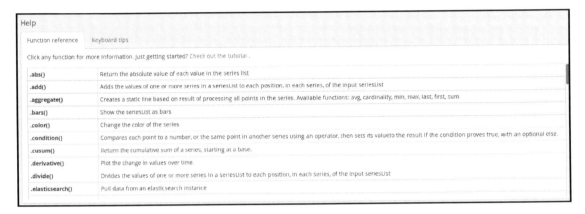

In the screenshot, we can see all available functions in Timelion and, by clicking on the function name, we can get the details, such as available parameters. We can chain these functions to get the desired visualization.

So, we will take the example of Metricbeat data, where we can get continuous system and process monitoring data that is quite easy to play around with in Timelion. We have already covered how to set up Metricbeat in the earlier chapter. Let's cover different functions available in Timelion, by means of which we can create interesting visualizations.

# .es() function

The `.es()` function is the shortcut of the `.elasticsearch()` function that fetches Elasticsearch data and plots it over the time interval. So, basically it fetches the time-series data and draws it against the time. It queries all the indices of Elasticsearch if we do not provide any specific index name. The `.es()` function shows the plot on the basis of the document count in the indices. The `.es()` function has different parameters that we can pass as per the requirements; each parameter has a name that we can mention inside the function. The parameter has a predefined format, which we need to follow only if we are not providing the name of the parameter. The `.es()` function has the following parameters:

- **q (for query):** Using the q parameter, we can add a query string to filter the data.
- **index:** Using the index parameter, we can specify the name of the index pattern to be used for the data plot. If we do not specify it, Elasticsearch will take data for all index patterns.
- **metric:** Using the metric parameter, we can apply different metrics such as sum, min, max, percentile, and so on on any field. We need to provide the metric name followed by the field name, for example `sum:system.memory.used.bytes`.
- **split:** The split parameter is used to split a field with a limit. For example, if we want to show the top five hostnames then we can pass it like this: `hostname:5`.
- **offset:** Using the offset parameter, we can retrieve the data based on the offset expression—for example, if we want to show data from the last day on the chart, which would appear as it is happening now. To show the data from the last day, we need to provide a-1d value for the offset
- **fit:** fit provides us the algorithm, by means of which we can fit the empty values using different options such as average, nearest, none or scale, and so on.
- **timefield:** The .es function picks the default time field for the index, which we can change by providing a timefield parameter to use for the *x* axis.

Let's say we want to plot a graph for the sum of memory used in bytes using Metricbeat data; then we need to write this expression:

```
.es(index=metricbeat*, metric='sum:system.memory.used.bytes')
```

In the expression, we have selected the index pattern **metricbeat\*** against the index parameter, and for the metric parameter, we have picked the `system.memory.used.bytes` field from the Metricbeat dataset. After executing the expression, we get the following graph:

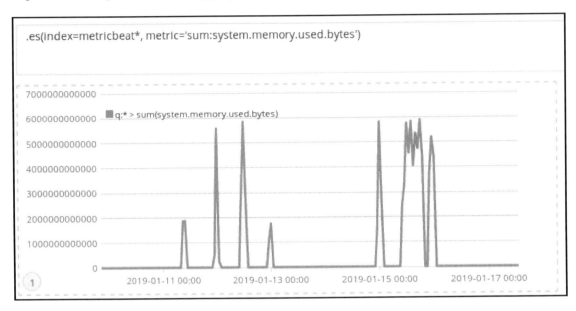

The previous diagram shows the graph using the Metricbeat index data for the sum of `'system.memory.used.bytes'`.

# .static() function

Using the `.static()` function, we can draw a static horizontal line on the chart with a given value. We can use this static line to show some sort of threshold on the graph. We can also use the label method to add a label for the added plot on the graph. The following graph shows the static line in red:

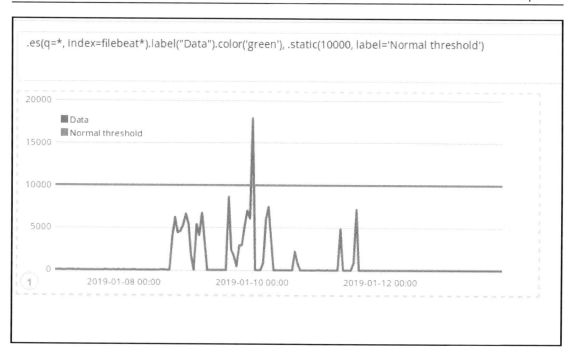

```
.es(q=*, index=filebeat*).label("Data").color('green'), .static(10000, label='Normal threshold')
```

The preceding graph is showing the filebeat data in green, where we are matching everything using the q=* query inside the .es() function. After that, we have added a static function to add the static horizontal line at value 10000 and provided the label **Normal threshold** just as an example. This way, in any graph, we can add the static horizontal line at any point using the .static() function.

# .bars() function

The bar representation of the time-series data. In the following graph, we have changed the view of the filebeat data line to bar by chaining the `.bar()` function at the end of the first expression:

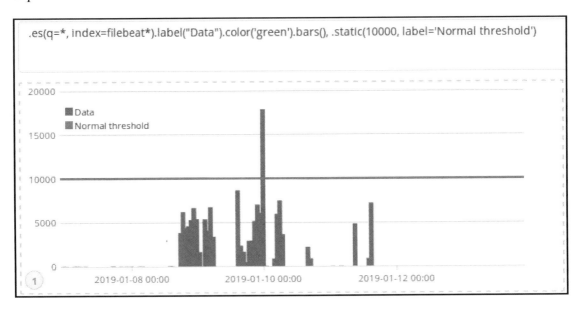

```
.es(q=*, index=filebeat*).label("Data").color('green').bars(), .static(10000, label='Normal threshold')
```

In the previous graph, the same filebeat data is now converted into a bar chart. We can chain the `.bars()` function to any Timelion expression to convert it into a bar chart.

# .points() function

If we want to change the chart-series display to points, then we can chain the `.points()` function with the expression. The following graph shows the same bar-chart data series with point representation:

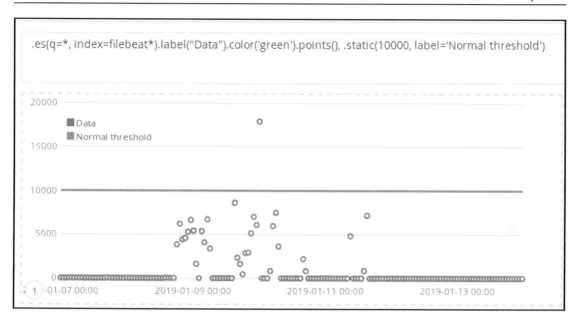

The graph shows the point display for the series.

# .color() function

Using the `.color()` function, we can change the color of any series. In the previous diagram, we used the `.color()` function to change the filebeat series color to green. Timelion automatically applies different colors for different expressions and we can change that color using the `.color()` function:

```
.es(q=*, index=filebeat*.color('green')
```

In the previous expression, we have applied the green color for the visualization plot using the `.color()` function.

# .derivative() function

Using the `.derivative()` function, we can plot the difference in value over time. It shows the derivative of a time series, which is the slope of the curve. The following example shows the derivative of the time series for filebeat data:

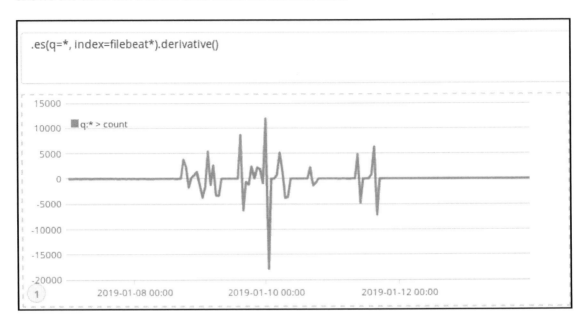

The graph is showing the derivative of the time series. We are using the same data that was plotted in the previous image.

# .label() function

Using the `.label()` function, we can change the label of a series. By using `%`, we can get the reference of the existing label. By default, Timelion shows the label using the given expression, which is quite difficult to understand sometimes on a graph, and, for that reason, the `.label()` function is important to add a meaningful label for the series:

```
.es(q=*, index=filebeat*).label("Data")
```

In the previous expression, we have added the label for the visualization plot.

# .range() function

Using the `.range()` function, we can set the graph between a minimum and maximum value by keeping the same shape. In the `.range()` function, we provide two parameters, min and max. See the following expression, where we are scaling the graph by providing the min and max value:

```
.es(q=*, index=filebeat*).label("Data").color('green').range(2000, 10000)
```

In the preceding expression, we have given the min value as `2000` and the max value as `10000`. After executing the preceding expression, we would get the following graph:

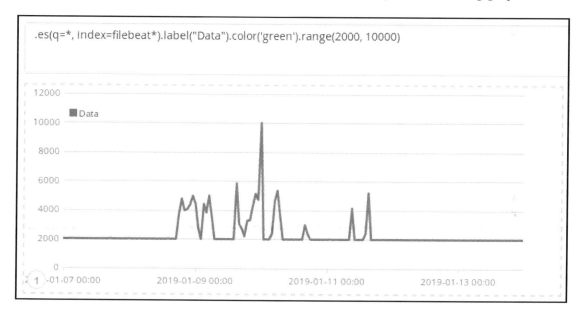

The previous diagram shows the same graph with a scaled view, where we have applied a range starting from `2000` and going up to `10000` using the `.range()` function.

# .holt() function

The `.holt()` function basically samples the series data from the beginning and then forecasts the future trend of series data using different optional parameters. We can also use it for anomaly detection. It has different parameters, such as alpha, which ranges from 0 to 1. If we increase the alpha value the new series will closely follow the original series, and if we lower the alpha value, it will make the series smoother. Then comes the beta, which also ranges from 0 to 1. Increasing it will make the rising/falling line longer while decreasing the beta value will make this learn the new trends quickly.

After beta, we have gamma, which also ranges from 0 to 1. If we increase it, it will give more importance to the recent reasons; if we lower it then it will give less importance to the recent series data and more importantly the historical data. Then we can provide the season like the duration to pick for repeating like 1w for one week. If we provide a season, then we can also set the last parameter, which is a sample to set the number of seasons to pick for data sampling. This expression shows a simple `.holt()` function implementation:

```
.es(q=*, index=filebeat*).label("Data").color('green').range(2000,
10000).holt(0.1,1)
```

The previous expression is showing the implementation of the `.holt()` function and, after executing this expression, we would get the following graph:

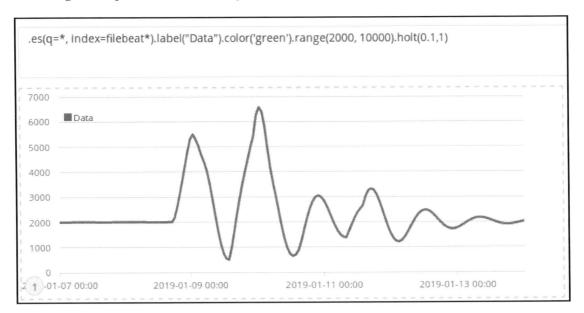

The preceding diagram is showing a smooth graph after applying the `.holt()` function. There are many more functions in Timelion that we can use to create a visualization using time-series data.

# Use cases of Timelion

There are different use cases where we can use Timelion, such as if we want to plot a graph with metrics of a certain field value. Using Timelion, we can plot a graph where, on the same axis, we can show the current data and historical data. This view helps us to track the difference quite easily. Timelion also provides the option to fetch data from different indices for a single visualization, meaning unlike Kibana Visualize, here we can refer multiple Elasticsearch indexes to create a single graph. It has different functions that can work together to create complex data visualizations that cannot be created in Kibana Visualize. Let's look at some examples one by one—we will see how Timelion can be used.

Let's look at an example of Metricbeat data. Suppose we want to see the sum of the total virtual memory the process has. To do that, we need to refer the field `system.process.memory.size` and to plot the graph we need to write the following expression:

```
.es(metric='sum:system.process.memory.size')
```

Using the previous expression, we can plot the line chart with the sum of total virtual memory of the process. If we want to change this to a bar chart, then we can simply use the add `.bars()` function after the expression:

```
.es(metric='sum:system.process.memory.size').bars()
```

In the same way, we can change it to a point chart by replacing `.bars()` with the `.points()` function.

If we want to see what the difference is in `system.memory.used.bytes` for today and the day before yesterday, then we can plot the graph with the current data and the day before yesterday's data by using the offset parameter of the `.es()` function. To plot this graph, we need to execute the following expression:

```
.es(metric='sum:system.memory.used.bytes', offset=-2d).color('blue'),
.es(metric='sum:system.memory.used.bytes').color('green')
```

After executing the expression, we would get the following graph:

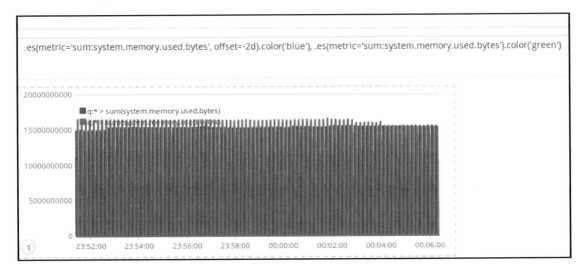

In the graph, we have the current data and two-day old data, which we are comparing on the same axis. The plots are overlapping and it is quite difficult to understand. To solve this issue, we can convert this line graph into a point graph by executing the following changed expression:

```
.es(metric='sum:system.memory.used.bytes',
offset=-2d).color('blue').points(),
.es(metric='sum:system.memory.used.bytes').color('green').points()
```

After executing the expression, we would get the following graph:

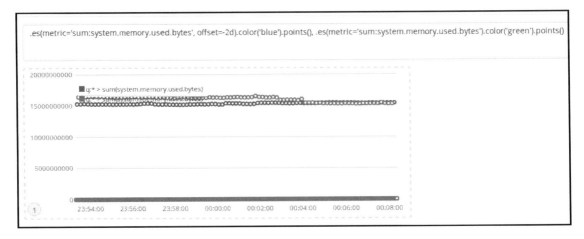

In the graph, we have a points representation of the data, which is now easy to interpret as there is no overlapping of plots. This way, we can apply the functions as per our requirements. If we want to see what the trend here is, then we can apply the `.trend()` function, which creates a plot for the trend using the regression algorithm. So, to apply the trend on the series, we need to modify the expression as follows:

```
.es(metric='sum:system.memory.used.bytes').color('green').trend()
```

After executing the expression, we get a trend plot showing the data trend based on history. The following diagram shows a plot with the current trend for the series:

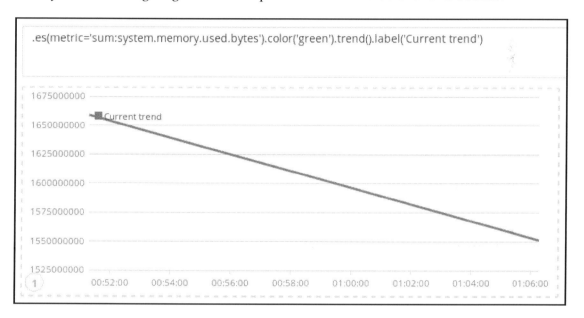

The graph is showing the trend going down. This trend can be created for any series just by chaining the expression with the `.trend()` function. If we are getting lots of spikes in a graph, then it is quite difficult to get an idea of how the data series is plotted. To solve this kind of issue, we can use the moving average function, which calculates the average of a series at a regular time interval and then plots the chart on the basis of the calculated value. Check out the expression:

```
.es(metric='sum:system.memory.used.bytes').color('green').mvavg(1m)
```

In the expression, we are creating a moving average with an interval of 1 minute. The following diagram shows the result of the expression's execution:

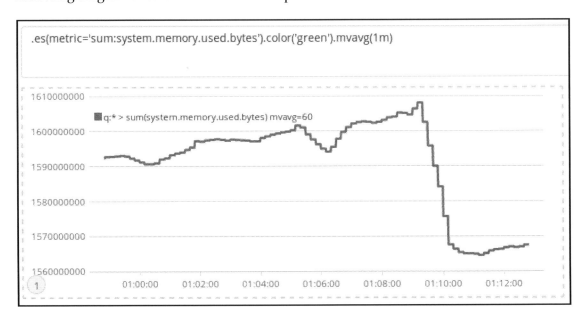

In the diagram, we can see that the data-series plot has smoothened and we can easily understand what is happening and how the data is flowing. In this way, we can use Timelion to get the answers to some complex questions, which is not possible under the Kibana Visualize option.

Once the Timelion graph has been created, we can save it by clicking on the **Save** link in the top-right menu options. This opens a screen with two options—the first is **Save entire Timelion sheet**, by means of which we can save the complete Timelion sheet, which can again be opened under Timelion. The second option, save the current expression as Kibana dashboard panel, saves the Timelion graph as a Kibana visualization, which can then be added to a Dashboard. After clicking on the desired option, we need to provide the name for the expression to save and then click on the save button to save.

# Dev Tools

Dev Tools provides us with the console option, from which we can execute Elasticsearch queries. We have two panes under the Dev Tools console, one for executing the queries and other to show the results of executed queries. The Dev Tools console provides us the type hint, which makes it quite easy to create an Elasticsearch query. We need to click on the Dev Tools link from the left menu option to open the Dev Tools page. See the following screenshot:

In the screenshot, under the console in the left pane, we can write Elasticsearch queries. After executing the query, the result is shown in the right pane.

Apart from the console, we have two other options under Dev Tools, Search Profiler and Grok Debugger. Using Search Profiler, we can profile any search query of Elasticsearch as it provides details of each query with a query duration for each component, along with the percentage of time consumed for each component. Using this method, we can optimize our queries.

Then we have Grok Debugger, by means of which we can create a Grok Pattern for any sample data. Here, we can put the sample data in the first text box, then, in the next text box, we can add the Grok Pattern, which matches the sample data and shows the structured data under the third text box. This Grok Pattern can be used to parse the actual data using Logstash.

# Console

Under the **Developer tools** | **Console**, we can execute Elasticsearch queries. From the Console, we can execute queries on any Elasticsearch index as **Developer tools Console** is not dependent on Kibana Index Patterns and can query an index that is available. The console has two panes—the left one is to execute the Elasticsearch query while the right one shows the responses to the query. First, we need to type the query; type hint helps us using auto-suggestion. Once the query is written, we can click on the **Click to send request** button that executes the query. Once the query has executed successfully we can get the response in the right pane of the Console. See the following screenshot:

The previous screenshot is showing the Elasticsearch query request and its response using Kibana Dev Tools Console.

We have a settings button in the request pane, under which we have different options such as copy as cURL, by means of which we can copy the query as a cURL request. Then we have a link, open documentation, to open the search documentation and lastly, we have the auto-indent option, by means of which we can indent the query.

# Search Profiler

We can profile our Elasticsearch queries under the Search Profiler option of Dev Tools. There are basically two panes—in the left pane we need to type the query and then click on the profile button. This will generate a Query Profile report where we can see the shard-wise details. See the following screenshot, where I have taken a query and generated the query profile:

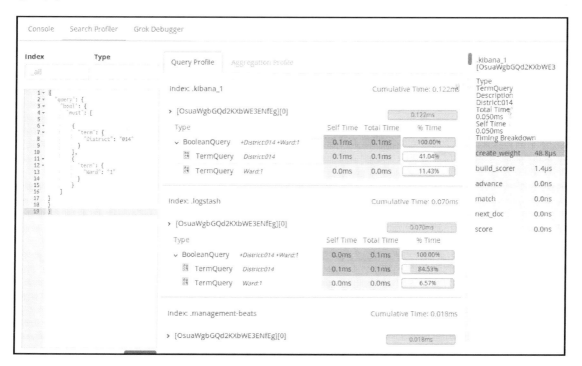

In the previous screenshot, we can see the first shard, where we have BooleanQuery, under which we have two instances of **TermQuery**. It shows the cumulative time of the query in ms with self-time and the total time with the percentage of the time. This way we can get the granular details for query execution and can tune it accordingly.

# Grok Debugger

Using Grok Debugger, we can create the pattern to parse any sample unstructured data, which can be a line of any log file or any file data. Once that unstructured data is parsed through the created pattern, we can generate the structured data, which can easily be analyzed in Elasticsearch using Kibana. For example, we might have the following sample data:

```
127.0.0.1 GET /index.php 11374 0.019
```

We can create a pattern like following to process it:

```
%{IP:client} %{WORD:method} %{URIPATHPARAM:request} %{NUMBER:bytes}
%{NUMBER:duration}
```

After simulating the Grok Pattern, we can convert the preceding sample unstructured data into structured data:

```
{
   "duration": "0.019",
   "request": "/index.php",
   "method": "GET",
   "bytes": "11374",
   "client": "127.0.0.1"
}
```

The following screenshot shows the preceding flow:

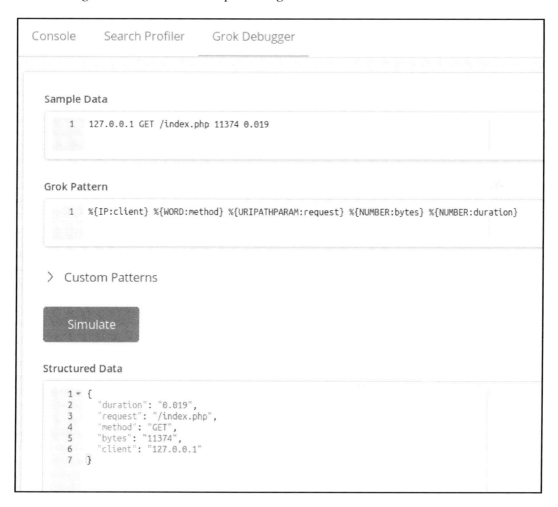

In the same way, we can parse any unstructured data using this Grok Debugger.

# Summary

So, in this chapter, we have covered Timelion and Dev Tools, which are quite useful tools of Kibana. We started with a Timelion introduction. Then we looked at the different functions that are available in Timelion, such as the `.es()` function to set the Elasticsearch data source, and its different parameters including index, metric, split, offset, fit and time field, and so on. After that, have covered other functions such as `.static()` to create a static line on the $x$ axis, the `.points()` function to convert the graph into a point display, `.color()` to change the color of the plot, the `.derivetive()` function to plot the difference in value over time, `.label()` to set the label for a data series, .range to limit the graph display between particular min and max ranges, and lastly the `.holt()` function to forecast the future trend or to get the anomaly in data. For a complete reference of functions, you can refer to the help section of Timelion. We also covered the use cases of Timelion.

After Timelion, we covered Dev Tools, by means of which we can do multiple things. After the Dev Tools introduction, we covered the different options of Dev Tools including the Console, by means of which we can execute Elasticsearch queries and can get the response on the same page. Then we covered the Search Profiler, by means of which we can profile any Elasticsearch query by getting the details of the query components. Lastly, we covered Grok Debugger, where we can create the Grok Pattern to parse sample data through which the unstructured sample data can be converted into structured data. This structured data then can be used for data analysis or visualization, and so on.

So, basically, in this book we have tried to cover all important aspects of Kibana along with the introduction of other components of Elastic Stack. We started with the installation, then we covered the data exploration; using Kibana, we saw our data in a raw form as it was coming from different sources. Once data was explored, we could visualize the data and we did it in a chapter where we have covered all about data visualization.

Then we covered X-Pack features and machine learning by creating jobs and analyzing them. After X-Pack, we covered APM. First, we went through the introduction and then covered the practical implementations of APM using the Django application. Finally, in this last chapter, we covered Kibana Advanced Tools, including Timelion and Dev Tools.

I hope this book has given you a basic understanding of Kibana. You may be able to start exploring your data now using Kibana. If you like the book, then do add your comments to the online platform so that other members can get an idea of the book.

# Other Books You May Enjoy

If you enjoyed this book, you may be interested in these other books by Packt:

**Mastering Elastic Stack**
Yuvraj Gupta

ISBN: 9781786460011

- Build a pipeline with help of Logstash and Beats to visualize Elasticsearch data in Kibana
- Use Beats to ship any type of data to the Elastic stack
- Understand Elasticsearch APIs, modules, and other advanced concepts
- Explore Logstash and it's plugins
- Discover how to utilize the new Kibana UI for advanced analytics
- See how to work with the Elastic Stack using other advanced configurations
- Customize the Elastic Stack and plugin development for each of the component
- Work with the Elastic Stack in a production environment
- Explore the various components of X-Pack in detail.

**Learning Elastic Stack 6.0**
Pranav Shukla

ISBN: 9781787281868

- Familiarize yourself with the different components of the Elastic Stack
- Get to know the new functionalities introduced in Elastic Stack 6.0
- Effectively build your data pipeline to get data from terabytes or petabytes of data into Elasticsearch and Logstash for searching and logging
- Use Kibana to visualize data and tell data stories in real-time
- Secure, monitor, and use the alerting and reporting capabilities of Elastic Stack
- Take your Elastic application to an on-premise or cloud-based production environment

# Leave a review - let other readers know what you think

Please share your thoughts on this book with others by leaving a review on the site that you bought it from. If you purchased the book from Amazon, please leave us an honest review on this book's Amazon page. This is vital so that other potential readers can see and use your unbiased opinion to make purchasing decisions, we can understand what our customers think about our products, and our authors can see your feedback on the title that they have worked with Packt to create. It will only take a few minutes of your time, but is valuable to other potential customers, our authors, and Packt. Thank you!

# Index

# D

dashboard
  configuring, with APM Server 123, 124
  creating 86, 87, 88, 89, 90
data table 78, 79
data visualization
  about 70
  area chart, creating 72, 73, 74
  data aggregation 70
  data table 78, 79
  heat map 74, 75
  metric 79, 80
  pie chart 76, 77
  Tag Cloud 81, 82
  types 71, 72
data, discovering
  about 54, 55
  expanded data view 56, 57
  field display, limiting 55, 56
data, dissecting
  about 57
  data, filtering 61, 62, 63
  data, searching with search bar 60, 61
  time filter 57
Debian package
  Elasticsearch, installing 22
  Kibana, installing 25
Dev Tools
  about 147, 148
  console 148, 149
  Grok Debugger 150, 151
  Search Profiler 149, 150
Django application
  configuring, with APM 125, 127, 128, 129, 130

# E

Elastic Stack, components
  Beats 10, 14
  Elasticsearch 10, 11
  Kibana 10, 13
  Logstash 10, 12
Elastic Stack, use cases
  about 17
  alerting 19

  application performance, monitoring 18
  data visualization 20
  log management 18
  monitoring 19
  security 19
  system performance, monitoring 18
Elastic Stack
  about 10
  Beats, installing 27
  Elasticsearch, installing 21
  installing 20
  Kibana, installing 24
  Logstash, installing 23
Elasticsearch, components
  cluster 12
  document 12
  index 12
  node 12
  shard 12
  type 12
Elasticsearch
  about 10, 11, 125
  installing 21
  installing, with Debian package 22
  installing, with Homebrew 21
  installing, with MSI Windows installer 21
  installing, with RPM package 22
  installing, with tar file 21
  reference 21

# F

field display
  available fields 55
  limiting 55, 56
  selected fields 55
Filebeat
  about 15
  configuring 33
  installing 29
filtered data, saving
  about 64
  saved searches, managing 66, 67
  search, saving 64, 65

split slices 70

# T

Tag Cloud 81, 82
tar file
  Elasticsearch, installing 21
time filter
  about 57
  absolute time range filter 59
  quick time range filter 58
  recent time range filter 60
  relative time range filter 58, 59
Timelion
  .bars() function 138
  .color() function 139
  .derivative() function 140
  .es() function 135, 136
  .holt() function 142, 143
  .label() function 140
  .points() function 138, 139
  .range() function 141
  .static() function 136, 137
  about 134
  use cases 143, 144, 145, 146
TShark 36

# U

universally unique identifier (UUID) 12

# V

visualization
  inspecting 82, 83
  sharing 83, 84, 85, 86

# W

Windows
  APM Server, installing 122, 123
  Kibana, installing 27
Winlogbeat 16

# X

X-Pack
  about 94
  alerting 102, 103, 104, 105, 106
  installation 94, 95, 96
  machine learning 108, 109
  monitoring 101, 102
  reporting 106, 107
  security 96

# Y

YUM Package Repositories
  using 24
YUM
  APM Server, installing 122

# Z

zypper
  using, on OpenSUSE-based distributions 26

Printed in Great Britain
by Amazon